DATE DUE

GAYLORD			PRINTED IN U.S.A

An introduction to econometrics

An introduction to econometrics

M. J. C. SURREY

CLARENDON PRESS · OXFORD
1974

Oxford University Press, Ely House, London W. 1

GLASGOW NEW YORK TORONTO MELBOURNE WELLINGTON
CAPE TOWN IBADAN NAIROBI DAR ES SALAAM LUSAKA ADDIS ABABA
DELHI BOMBAY CALCUTTA MADRAS KARACHI LAHORE DACCA
KUALA LUMPUR SINGAPORE HONG KONG TOKYO

CASEBOUND ISBN 0 19 877048 0
PAPERBACK ISBN 0 19 877048 9

© OXFORD UNIVERSITY PRESS 1974

Set by The Pitman Press, Bath
Printed in Great Britain
by J. W. Arrowsmith Ltd., Bristol

Preface

The aim of this little book is to give, as briefly as possible, an account of the main aspects of classical regression analysis without using matrix algebra but also without asking the reader to take results on trust. It is hoped that this will make it useful to two kinds of reader. First, students who intend to pursue econometrics in greater depth may find it helpful to gain some knowledge of econometric problems without at the same time having to master unfamiliar algebraic methods. Secondly, working economists in almost every field nowadays need at least to be able to assess the empirical evidence deployed by their colleagues, without necessarily wishing to become practising econometricians themselves. Such economists will generally know something of the significance of R^2 as a measure of goodness-of-fit and of the meaning of the standard error of a coefficient, but talk of, for example, simultaneous equation bias or the asymptotic properties of estimators may find them a little less certain. The assumption of most econometrics texts is that the convenience of matrix algebra makes its comprehension a *sine qua non* for intending econometricians. This may make such information inaccessible to those whose interest is only occasional, yet who may feel uneasy about taking too many econometric assertions on trust.

I am greatly indebted to Gerhard Stuvel, who encouraged me in my belief that a short book of this kind would be useful, read the manuscript, and made a number of valuable suggestions. My debt to the authors of more advanced texts is, of course, formidable; it is only inadequately recognized in the references given as suggested further reading at the end of each chapter.

I gratefully acknowledge the permission of the Biometrika Trustees to reprint tables 3 and 4. I am also indebted to the Literary Executor of the late Sir Ronald A. Fisher, F.R.S., to Dr Frank Yates, F.R.S., and to Longman Group Ltd., London, for permission to reprint tables 1 and 2 from their book *Statistical Tables for Biological, Agricultural and Medical Research.*

Oxford,   M.J.C.S.
June 1973

Contents

Basic concepts

1.1. Econometrics is the art of confronting the *a priori* reasoning of the economic theorist with the statistical evidence which is available. The kinds of results which can be obtained, and the kinds of problems which may arise, can most easily be illustrated with a simple example. Keynes suggested that consumption would depend primarily on the level of income; formally:

$$C_t = f(Y_t), \tag{1.1}$$

where C_t is the level of consumption at time t and Y_t is the level of income. The first problem confronting the econometrician is that of specifying the mathematical form of the general function (1.1). Suppose it to be linear:

$$C_t = \alpha + \beta Y_t. \tag{1.2}$$

Then the next step is to try to find the values of α and β which describe the available data on consumption and income as well as possible.

1.2. Since the hypothesis is that income is the most important, not the only, relevant determinant, consumption at any time will in reality be influenced by a host of other factors which are omitted from eqn (1.2). If the data are graphed, one would expect to find a scatter of points not lying exactly on any straight line (Fig. 1.1). Clearly, in some sense AA is a better fit to the data than BB, but even the best possible straight line will not 'explain' all the variation in consumption. The variation in C_t which remains even when the best possible allowance is made for the influence of income may arise from the effect of other variables which for the sake of simplicity have been neglected, or from an irreducible element of randomness in human behaviour, or from errors in observing or measuring consumption.

An important point which follows from this is that any set of data which is available is in principle only one possible drawing from a theoretically infinite population. National income was at a certain level in one year, and the level of consumption in that year was measured. But even if we knew the 'true' relationship between consumption and income, if income is at the same level this year consumption may be at a different level for any or all of the reasons just mentioned. Thus as well as estimating α and β in eqn (1.2), one is likely to want to

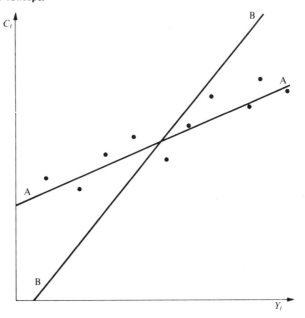

Fig. 1.1. Two possible lines through a data scatter

know by how much consumption might reasonably depart from the 'predicted' level because of the 'error term'.

1.3. Following on from this, a different sample of data might in principle have been available. This would have given rise to different estimates of α and β. Yet both sets of estimates purport to be estimates of the 'true' relationship, so any particular estimates must be accompanied by some assessment of the probability that they are close to the unknown true parameters.

1.4. A second way of looking at at least part of econometrics is to see it as a way of coping with the near-impossibility in economics of conducting a controlled experiment. Suppose that the level of investment is thought, *a priori*, to depend in a linear way on the rate of change of output and on the level of the interest rate:

$$I_t = \alpha + \beta \Delta X_t + \gamma r_t$$

where I_t is the level of investment, ΔX_t is the change in output and r_t is the interest rate, all in period t.

The most obvious way to estimate the coefficient of the change in output would clearly be to hold the interest rate constant and to examine the behaviour of investment as the change in output varies, and vice versa for the influence of the interest rate. Economists can of course do this in their theoretical work — the prevalence of the '*ceteris paribus*' clause evidences as much – but since data cannot be generated at will under the required conditions, it is not a technique which is much use in empirical economics. What can be done, however, is to calculate the correlations between I_t and ΔX_t, forgetting about variations in r_t, and between I_t and r_t, forgetting about variations in ΔX_t and then to 'correct' these correlations for the correlation between the explanatory variables ΔX_t and r_t. This is, very loosely, what the technique of multiple regression does. This way of approaching the problem immediately suggests what is at once the most pervasive and the least tractable of econometric problems – that of multicollinearity (or, more generally, of identification). Suppose that ΔX_t and r_t are always highly correlated, so that whenever ΔX_t is high, so is r_t, and vice-versa. It may then be very difficult to disentangle their separate influences on investment and – intuitively – it is clear that this problem is, in the end, insoluble.

1.5. Before embarking on the investigation of the kinds of problems outlined above, it may be useful to provide very simple explanations of some of the terms and algebraic techniques which will be used extensively in what follows.

We shall frequently need to consider, and manipulate, sums of terms. To avoid writing them out in full, the Σ notation is used. Thus if we have a time-series of values of a variable X_t, where t covers, say, 20 periods, we write

$$X_1 + X_2 + X_3 + \ldots + X_{20} \quad \text{as} \quad \sum_{t=1}^{20} X_t$$

or, if we have in general n observations, as $\sum_{t=1}^{n} X_t$. The range of summation, 1 to n, is often omitted for clarity of notation where there is no ambiguity, i.e. ΣX_t.

Manipulations of sums can, until the notation becomes familiar, always be checked by writing out the first few terms. Thus, for example,

$$\left(\sum_{t=1}^{n} X_t \right)^2 = (X_1 + X_2 + \ldots + X_n)^2$$
$$= (X_1^2 + X_2^2 + \ldots + 2X_1 X_2 + 2X_1 X_3 + \ldots + 2X_2 X_3 + \ldots)$$
$$= \Sigma X_t^2 + 2\Sigma X_s X_t \quad s, t = 1 \ldots n, s < t.$$

Suppose that an experiment is conducted in which a number of different outcomes are possible, each having a known probability of occurring. If the experiment were repeated an infinite number of times, the average result would be the sum of the value of each outcome multiplied by the probability of its happening. Thus if a die is thrown, the average count over a large number of throws will be

$$1 \times \frac{1}{6} + 2 \times \frac{1}{6} + \ldots + 6 \times \frac{1}{6} = 3 \cdot 5$$

since the probability of each score is $\frac{1}{6}$ (provided that the die is unbiased). This average can be termed the *expected value* of a single throw. In general, if there is a discrete variable X with a known probability function $f(X)$, the expected value of X is

$$E(X) = \sum_{i=1}^{n} X_i f(X_i).$$

This is a weighted sum of all the values taken by X, where the weights are the probabilities of each value's occurring. In the case of the die, $f(X) = \frac{1}{6}$ for all values of X.

It follows directly that the expected value of X, being the weighted average of possible values of X, is equal to the mean μ of the population from which X is drawn:

$$E(X) = \mu.$$

The expected value of a constant is, of course, the constant itself.

We shall also be interested in how 'spread out' the possible values of X are about the expected value. One measure of this will be a weighted average of the squared deviations from the expected value, the weights again being the probabilities of each value's occurring. This measure is known as the *variance* of X:

$$\text{var}(X) = \sum_{i=1}^{n} \{X_i - E(X_i)\}^2 f(X)$$

or

$$\text{var}(X) = E\{X_i - E(X_i)\}^2$$

$$= E(X_i - \mu)^2$$

since

$$E(X_i) = \mu.$$

1.6. It is necessary to mention briefly a few terms which are in frequent use to describe the *econometric properties of estimators*. Suppose we wish to obtain estimates of the parameters α and β in the true but unknown relationship $Y = \alpha + \beta X$. By some means or other we obtain an estimate, $\hat{\beta}$, of β, based on a sample of data on X and Y. What are the econometric properties of $\hat{\beta}$? First, except by chance, $\hat{\beta}$ will not be an absolutely exact measure of the true value β. There will be a *sampling error* of $(\hat{\beta} - \beta)$ which will differ from sample to sample, since each sample will give a different estimate of $\hat{\beta}$. Secondly, the method which is used tq obtain the estimate of $\hat{\beta}$ may lead to *bias*. This means that, for one reason or another, no matter how large the data sample or how many samples we use, $\hat{\beta}$ will *on average* differ from the true value β. In other words, the expected value of $\hat{\beta}$ will not be equal to β. The bias is $\{E(\hat{\beta}) - \beta\}$. Thirdly, we are likely to be interested in the dispersion of different values of $\hat{\beta}$ which might be obtained from different samples – that is, in the variance of $\hat{\beta}$:

$$\text{var}(\hat{\beta}) = E\{\hat{\beta} - E(\hat{\beta})\}^2.$$

If, of two methods of estimating $\hat{\beta}$, one method gives a lower variance of $\hat{\beta}$, that method is said to be more *efficient*.

Note that it is always assumed that there *is* a unique true value of a parameter. The econometrician is confronted with a particular set of data with which to make an estimate of the parameter. In principle, this set of data is only one among many which might have been used, each of which would have given a different estimate. Thus a particular estimate $\hat{\beta}$ must always be thought of as one drawing from a whole distribution. The less spread out this distribution (the smaller its variance), the more likely it is that the particular estimate which is in fact obtained will be close to the expected value of $\hat{\beta}$, which in turn will be equal to the true value β if the method of estimation (or *estimator*, for short) is unbiased.

Clearly both bias and efficiency are problems to the economist, who needs to speculate about the size of the particular sampling error $(\hat{\beta} - \beta)$, where β is unknown. This sampling error may easily be greater in the case of an unbiased but inefficient estimator than in the case of a biased but efficient estimator. It is impossible to say in general that unbiasedness is more important than efficiency, or vice-versa. This question is evaded by some econometricians who define the class of efficient estimators to include *only* unbiased ones. In the sort of case just outlined, this makes efficiency an unhelpful concept.

One possible judgement is to say that it is the expected *mean square error* (MSE) of an estimator which is important. The MSE will take account of both bias and variance, for

$$MSE = (\hat{\beta} - \beta)^2$$

and
$$E(MSE) = E(\hat{\beta} - \beta)^2$$

$$= E\{\hat{\beta} - E(\hat{\beta}) + E(\hat{\beta}) - \beta\}^2$$

$$= E\{\hat{\beta} - E(\hat{\beta})\}^2 + \{E(\hat{\beta}) - \beta\}^2 + 2E\{\hat{\beta} - E(\hat{\beta})\}\{E(\hat{\beta}) - \beta\}$$

$$= \text{var}(\hat{\beta}) + (\text{bias})^2$$

since $2E\{\hat{\beta} - E(\hat{\beta})\}\{E(\hat{\beta}) - \beta\}$

$$= 2\left[\{E(\hat{\beta})\}^2 - \{E(\hat{\beta})\}^2 - \beta E(\hat{\beta}) + \beta E(\hat{\beta})\right]$$

$$= 0.$$

1.7. Some of these properties of estimators can be examined for their behaviour as the size of the data sample approaches infinity. For example, it is possible to find cases where an estimator is biased for finite sample sizes, but where the bias diminishes as the sample size increases and vanishes as the size reaches infinity. Such an estimator is said to be *asymptotically unbiased*. If the variance of the estimator tends to zero as the sample size tends to infinity, it is said to be *asymptotically efficient*. If the estimator has both these properties, so that the estimate of β collapses on to the true value as the sample size reaches infinity, it is said to be *consistent*.

Despite the large amount of time devoted to the exploration of asymptotic properties by econometricians, their usefulness to most economists is clearly limited, given the rarity in economics of samples of near-infinite size. There are, of course, cases in which asymptotic properties may be relevant. It may be useful to know that an estimator is asymptotically biased if one would otherwise have devoted effort to increasing the sample size in the hope of eliminating bias. In one or two special cases, it may be possible to find the asymptotic variance of an estimator even though the actual variance cannot be derived; the former can then be used to make inferences about the latter.

1.8. Finally, it may be worth mentioning some of the more obvious limitations of econometrics. Perhaps the most fundamental is that measurement is not always possible. To take an obvious example, a great deal of economic theory depends on the notion of expectations: one aspect of a dynamic equilibrium is that it is a state in which expectations are fulfilled. But expectations (and 'animal spirits' and 'confidence') are not measurable, at least directly. The empirically-minded economist then has three alternatives. First, he may regard the theory as untestable. Secondly, he may hypothesize some mechanism which purports to show how expectations are generated from experience: for example, he may suggest that the expected level of a variable is based on the assumption that the growth rate in the current period will be maintained in the next period, so that

$$\frac{X_{t+1}^e - X_t}{X_t} = \frac{X_t - X_{t-1}}{X_{t-1}}$$

Then X_{t+1}^e, the expected level in the next period, can be expressed in terms of the current level, X_t, and the previous period's level, X_{t-1}, on which data are available. Thirdly, he may be able to ask people directly what their expectations are. Surveys of investment intentions conducted by the government or by the Confederation of British Industry are an example.

Expectations are not the only kind of 'variable' which may be difficult to measure: the concepts of permanent income and of the differing 'strengths' of incomes policy are two examples from fields in which a great deal of empirical work has been attempted.

The imputation of causality in econometrics needs some care. The confusion of correlation with causation is too notorious to need re-emphasis, but a number of terms used in econometrics need, almost always, to be read with implicit inverted commas in mind. For example, in writing

$$Y_t = \alpha + \beta X_t + u_t$$

it is conventional to speak of Y as the 'dependent' and X as the 'independent' variable and the estimated equation is said to 'explain' or 'account for' a certain proportion of the variation in Y. In what follows, terms such as these will be used on the grounds of convention and brevity, but the dangers of interpreting them literally should not be forgotten.

The need for the correct specification of a model and the need for reliable data with which to estimate it may seem to obvious to mention. But the fact that, in particular, the estimation of linear relationships is very much easier than that of non-linear forms, and the temptation to believe that any numerical estimate is better than no numerical estimate, combine to generate a very potent tendency towards 'naive quantification'. To take an extreme example, in the national accounts of Ceylon, value added by the construction industry is largely estimated as a constant multiple (4·25) of imports of construction materials. An 'import function' which sought to explain changes in imports of construction materials as a linear function of changes in the value added in the construction industry would fit very satisfactorily. But neither the linearity nor the goodness of fit would reflect any real economic phenomenon. (This example is taken from the paper by Shourie listed under *Further reading* below.)

Further reading

On the purpose and meaning of regression analysis, see:
C. F. Christ, *Econometric models and methods*, Chapter I. Wiley, New York (1966).

On the properties of estimators, see:
C. F. Christ, *op. cit.*, Chapter VII.

On the interpretation of regression equations, see:
A. S. Goldberger, *Topics in regression analysis*. Macmillan, New York (1968), and, for a disenchanted view,
A. Shourie, The use of macro-economic regression models of developing countries for forecasts and policy prescriptions: some reflections on current practice, *Oxford Economic Papers* (March 1972).

2 | Simple regression and correlation

2.1. The simplest relationship between two variables X and Y is the linear one

$$Y = \alpha + \beta X.$$

We have already pointed out that, for a variety of reasons, any actual data are unlikely to lie exactly on this line, but will rather be described by

$$Y_i = \alpha + \beta X_i + u_i, \qquad i = 1, 2, \ldots n$$

where u_i represents the 'error' or 'disturbance' associated with each observation. Note that u_i in this relationship can be either an equation error, representing the influence of omitted variables or randomness of behaviour, or an error in measuring Y (or both) but not an error in measuring X. It is then effectively assumed that the X_i are fixed values, in the sense that *in principle* the sample could be repeated with the same X_i but different u_i and hence different Y_i. If measurement error in X were the source of the disturbance, the true relationship would be

$$Y_i = \alpha + \beta X_i',$$

where X_i' is the true value of X_i. We actually observe

$$X_i = X_i' + u_i$$

so that

$$Y_i = \alpha + \beta(X_i - u_i)$$

or

$$Y_i = \alpha + \beta X_i - \beta u_i.$$

In this case, the disturbance term is not independent of the values of X_i. This causes complications which are dealt with later (Chapter 5).

2.2. We thus have a set of pairs of values of X and Y which will not lie exactly on any straight line. The problem is to find the 'best' line through the points.

Now *any* straight line through the scatter can be written as

$$\hat{Y}_i = \hat{\alpha} + \hat{\beta} X_i.$$

$\hat{Y}_i$ is the value of Y given by this line for each value of X_i. The difference between Y_i, the observed value of Y, and $\hat{Y}_i$ may be denoted by e_i, so that

$$e_i = Y_i - \hat{Y}_i = Y_i - \hat{\alpha} - \hat{\beta} X_i.$$

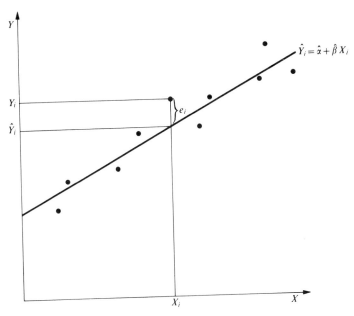

Fig. 2.1. The error term

Different lines drawn through the scatter will have different $\hat{\alpha}$ and $\hat{\beta}$, though the data, X_i and Y_i, are unchanged, and will thus result in a different set of values of e_i. The *least squares* criterion is that the 'best' line though the scatter is that one which minimizes the sum of squared residuals e_i. Denoting this sum by S, we thus have to minimize

$$S = \sum_{i=1}^{n} e_i^2 = \sum_{i=1}^{n} (Y_i - \hat{\alpha} - \hat{\beta} X_i)^2$$

with respect to the two variables $\hat{\alpha}$ and $\hat{\beta}$. Although we normally think of X and Y as variables and α and β as parameters, in this case we have *given* values of X and Y and we are *varying* $\hat{\alpha}$ and $\hat{\beta}$ to generate different lines. The justification of the least squares criterion is developed below (§2.6).

Thus we differentiate S partially with respect to $\hat{\alpha}$ and $\hat{\beta}$ and set the results equal to zero:

$$\frac{\partial S}{\partial \hat{\alpha}} = -2\Sigma(Y_i - \hat{\alpha} - \hat{\beta} X_i) = 0,$$

$$\frac{\partial S}{\partial \hat{\beta}} = -2\Sigma X_i(Y_i - \hat{\alpha} - \hat{\beta} X_i) = 0.$$

On simplification, these reduce to the so-called *normal equations* for a straight line:

$$\Sigma Y_i = n\hat{\alpha} + \hat{\beta}\Sigma X_i,$$

$$\Sigma X_i Y_i = \hat{\alpha}\Sigma X_i + \hat{\beta}\Sigma X_i^2.$$

Since ΣX_i, ΣY_i, $\Sigma X_i Y_i$, and ΣX_i^2 can be calculated from the data, and n is the number of observations, these two equations can be solved for $\hat{\alpha}$ and $\hat{\beta}$.

Note, though, that on dividing through the first normal equation by n, we obtain

$$\Sigma Y_i/n = \hat{\alpha} + \hat{\beta}\Sigma X_i/n$$

or
$$\overline{Y} = \hat{\alpha} + \hat{\beta}\overline{X},$$

where $\overline{Y}$ and $\overline{X}$ are the arithmetic means of the Y_i and X_i respectively; the least squares line must pass through the point $(\overline{X}, \overline{Y})$. Subtracting this from the original equation for the line

$$\hat{Y}_i = \hat{\alpha} + \hat{\beta}X_i,$$

we have
$$\hat{Y}_i - \overline{Y} = \hat{\beta}(X_i - \overline{X})$$

or
$$\hat{y}_i = \hat{\beta}x_i,$$

using the conventional method of denoting deviations of a variable from its mean value by lower case letters. It follows that

$$S = \Sigma e_i^2 = \Sigma(y_i - \hat{y}_i)^2$$

$$= \Sigma(y_i - \hat{\beta}x_i)^2$$

and
$$\frac{\partial S}{\partial \hat{\beta}} = -2\Sigma x_i(y_i - \hat{\beta}x_i).$$

Setting this equal to zero and solving for $\hat{\beta}$ gives

$$\hat{\beta} = \frac{\Sigma x_i y_i}{\Sigma x_i^2} \tag{2.1}$$

The ordinary least squares (OLS) estimate $\hat{\beta}$ can thus be obtained without the need to solve two simultaneous equations in $\hat{\alpha}$ and $\hat{\beta}$ if the data are expressed in deviation form; $\hat{\alpha}$ can then be calculated using the fact that the lines passes through the point of means, so that

$$\hat{\alpha} = \overline{Y} - \hat{\beta}\overline{X}.$$

2.3. We now inquire into the econometric properties of these OLS estimators $\hat{\alpha}$ and $\hat{\beta}$, that is, into their relationship to the true but unknown parameters α and β. Taking $\hat{\beta}$ first, we have

$$\hat{\beta} = \frac{\Sigma x_i y_i}{\Sigma x_i^2}.$$

Now we wish to relate $\hat{\beta}$ to β, the true value, which may be introduced by substituting for y_i the true relationship. Since

$$Y_i = \alpha + \beta X_i + u_i,$$

on taking deviations from means

$$y_i = \beta x_i + (u_i - \bar{u})$$

and thus

$$\hat{\beta} = \frac{\Sigma x_i(\beta x_i + u_i - \bar{u})}{\Sigma x_i^2}$$

$$= \beta + \frac{\Sigma x_i u_i}{\Sigma x_i^2} - \frac{\Sigma x_i \bar{u}}{\Sigma x_i^2} \qquad (2.2)$$

On taking expectations,

$$E(\hat{\beta}) = \beta + E\left[\frac{\Sigma x_i u_i}{\Sigma x_i^2}\right] - \frac{\bar{u}\Sigma x_i}{\Sigma x_i^2}$$

Now provided that $E(u_i)$ is a constant,

$$E(\hat{\beta}) = \beta + E(u_i)\frac{\Sigma x_i}{\Sigma x_i^2} - \frac{\bar{u}\Sigma x_i}{\Sigma x_i^2}$$

$$= \beta,$$

since $\qquad \Sigma x_i = \Sigma(X_i - \bar{X}) = \Sigma X_i - n(1/n)\Sigma X_i = 0.$

In practice, it is usually assumed that $E(u_i)$ is not only a constant, but zero. The true errors are assumed to be randomly drawn from a population with zero mean.

Thus $E(\hat{\beta}) = \beta$; the OLS estimator is unbiased.

The variance of $\hat{\beta}$ is by definition

$$\text{var}(\hat{\beta}) = E\{\hat{\beta} - E(\hat{\beta})\}^2$$

$$= E(\hat{\beta} - \beta)^2$$

since we have just proved that $E(\hat{\beta}) = \beta$. From eqn (2.2), since

$$\Sigma x_i \bar{u} = \bar{u}\Sigma x_i = 0,$$

$$\hat{\beta} - \beta = \frac{\Sigma x_i u_i}{\Sigma x_i^2}$$

and thus

$$\text{var}(\hat{\beta}) = E\left[\frac{\Sigma x_i u_i}{\Sigma x_i^2}\right]^2$$

$$= \left(\frac{1}{\Sigma x_i^2}\right)^2 E(x_1^2 u_1^2 + x_2^2 u_2^2 + \ldots + 2x_1 x_2 u_1 u_2 + \ldots).$$

If $E(u_i^2) = \sigma^2$, that is, if the variance of the true disturbances is a constant, σ^2, then $E(x_1^2 u_1^2 + x_2^2 u_2^2 + \ldots) = \sigma^2 \Sigma x_i^2$. Furthermore, if the true disturbances are genuinely random, and are thus uncorrelated with one another, then $E(u_i u_j) = 0$ $(i \neq j)$. Thus

$$\text{var}(\hat{\beta}) = \frac{\sigma^2}{\Sigma x_i^2}$$

Thus if
$$E(u_i) = 0$$

and
$$E(u_i u_j) = \sigma^2, \ i = j$$

$$= 0, \ \ i \neq j$$

then the OLS estimator $\hat{\beta}$ is an unbiased estimator of β with variance $\sigma^2(\hat{\beta}) = \sigma^2/\Sigma x_i^2$.

2.4. For $\hat{\alpha}$, we have

$$\hat{\alpha} = \overline{Y} - \hat{\beta}\overline{X}$$

$$= \frac{1}{n}\Sigma Y_i - \hat{\beta}\overline{X}$$

$$= \frac{1}{n}\Sigma(\alpha + \beta X_i + u_i) - \hat{\beta}\overline{X}$$

$$= \alpha + \beta\overline{X} - \hat{\beta}\overline{X} + \frac{1}{n}\Sigma u_i \qquad (2.3)$$

and
$$E(\hat{\alpha}) = \alpha$$

since
$$E(\hat{\beta}) = \beta \quad \text{and} \quad E(u_i) = 0.$$

For the variance of $\hat{\alpha}$, from eqn (2.3)

$$\hat{\alpha} - \alpha = -\overline{X}(\hat{\beta} - \beta) + \frac{1}{n}\Sigma u_i$$

and thus
$$\text{var}(\hat{\alpha}) = E\{\hat{\alpha} - E(\hat{\alpha})\}^2$$

$$= E(\hat{\alpha} - \alpha)^2$$

$$= E\{\overline{X}^2(\hat{\beta} - \beta)^2 - \frac{2\overline{X}}{n}(\hat{\beta} - \beta)\Sigma u_i + \frac{1}{n^2}(\Sigma u_i)^2\}$$

$$= \overline{X}^2 \text{var}(\hat{\beta}) + \frac{\sigma^2}{n}$$

since
$$E(u_i) = 0$$

and
$$E(\Sigma u_i)^2 = E(u_1 + u_2 + \ldots)^2$$

$$= E(u_1^2 + u_2^2 + \ldots + 2u_1 u_2 \ldots)$$

$$= n\sigma^2.$$

Thus
$$\operatorname{var}(\hat{\alpha}) = \overline{X}^2\,\frac{\sigma^2}{\Sigma x_i^2} + \frac{\sigma^2}{n}\,.$$

$$= \sigma^2\left(\frac{X^2}{\Sigma x_i^2} + \frac{1}{n}\right)$$

2.5. For the covariance of $\hat{\alpha}$ and $\hat{\beta}$ we have

$$\operatorname{covar}(\hat{\alpha},\hat{\beta}) = E\{\hat{\alpha} - E(\hat{\alpha})\}\{\hat{\beta} - E(\hat{\beta})\}$$

$$= E\{-\overline{X}(\hat{\beta} - \beta) + \frac{1}{n}\Sigma u_i\}\{\hat{\beta} - \beta\}$$

$$= -\overline{X}\,E(\hat{\beta} - \beta)^2 + E\left[\frac{1}{n}\Sigma u_i\,\frac{\Sigma x_i}{\Sigma x_i^2}\right]$$

$$= -\overline{X}\,\operatorname{var}(\hat{\beta}) + \frac{1}{n}\sigma^2\,\frac{\Sigma x_i}{\Sigma x_i^2}$$

$$= -\overline{X}\,\operatorname{var}(\hat{\beta})$$

since $\Sigma x_i = 0.$

Thus
$$\operatorname{covar}(\hat{\alpha},\hat{\beta}) = -\overline{X}\,\frac{\sigma^2}{\Sigma x_i^2}$$

As is to be expected, the covariance between $\hat{\alpha}$ and $\hat{\beta}$ will be negative if $\overline{X}$ is positive; if the data give us an overestimate of β, we should expect this to result in an underestimate of α.

2.6. It is straightforward, though tedious, to justify the use of the least squares criterion by showing that it provides the best linear unbiased estimator (BLUE) of β.

The class of linear estimators (linear, that is, in the observations Y_i which we are trying to 'explain') is

$$b = \Sigma a_i Y_i,$$

where the a_i are weights to be chosen. Now

$$E(b) = E(\Sigma a_i Y_i)$$

$$= \Sigma a_i E(Y_i),$$

since the a_i are fixed weights.

Therefore,
$$E(b) = \Sigma a_i(\alpha + \beta X_i)$$

since
$$E(Y_i) = E(\alpha + \beta X_i + u_i)$$

$$= \alpha + \beta X_i$$

because $$E(u_i) = 0.$$

Thus $$E(b) = \alpha\Sigma a_i + \beta\Sigma a_i X_i$$

and, for b to be unbiased, this must equal β, so we require that

$$\Sigma a_i = 0 \quad \text{and} \quad \Sigma a_i X_i = 1.$$

These conditions will be satisfied by all linear unbiased estimators; we wish to find the best of these, that is, the one with minimum variance. Now

$$\text{var}(b) = \text{var}(\Sigma a_i Y_i)$$
$$= E\{\Sigma a_i Y_i - E(\Sigma a_i Y_i)\}^2$$
$$= E[\Sigma a_i\{Y_i - E(Y_i)\}]^2$$
$$= E(\Sigma a_i u_i)^2$$
$$= \sigma^2\Sigma a_i^2,$$

since $$Y_i - E(Y_i) = u_i, \quad E(u_i^2) = \sigma^2,$$

and $$E(u_i u_j) = 0, (i \neq j).$$

We thus have to minimize $\sigma^2\Sigma a_i^2$ or (what comes to the same thing, since σ^2 is a constant) Σa_i^2, subject to the two earlier conditions, namely (a), $\Sigma a_i = 0$ and (b), $\Sigma a_i X_i = 1$. Form the Lagrangean

$$\mathcal{L} = \Sigma a_i^2 - \lambda_1\Sigma a_i - \lambda_2(\Sigma a_i X_i - 1).$$

Differentiating partially with respect to each a_i, and setting the result equal to zero gives

$$\frac{\partial\mathcal{L}}{\partial a_i} = 2a_i - \lambda_1 - \lambda_2 X_i = 0 \tag{2.4}$$

or $$a_i = \frac{1}{2}(\lambda_1 + \lambda_2 X_i).$$

Substituting in the two constraints:

(a) $$\frac{1}{2}(n\lambda_1 + \lambda_2\Sigma X_i) = 0$$

(b) $$\frac{1}{2}(\lambda_1\Sigma X_i + \lambda_2\Sigma X_i^2) = 1.$$

Hence from (a),

$$\lambda_1 = -\frac{\lambda_2}{n}\Sigma X_i$$

and thus substituting in (b),

$$-\frac{\lambda_2}{n}(\Sigma X_i)^2 + \lambda_2\Sigma X_i^2 = 2.$$

Thus
$$\lambda_2 = \frac{2n}{n\Sigma X_i^2 - (\Sigma X_i)^2}$$

$$= \frac{2}{\Sigma x_i^2}$$

since
$$\Sigma x_i^2 = \Sigma(X_i - \bar{X})^2$$
$$= n\Sigma X_i^2 - (\Sigma X_i)^2,$$

and
$$\lambda_1 = \frac{2\Sigma X_i}{n\Sigma x_i^2}$$

$$= -\frac{2\bar{X}}{\Sigma x_i^2}.$$

From eqn (2.4),
$$a_i = \frac{1}{2}(\lambda_1 + \lambda_2 X_i),$$

and thus
$$a_i = -\frac{\bar{X}}{\Sigma x_i^2} + \frac{X_i}{\Sigma x_i^2}$$

$$= \frac{x_i}{\Sigma x_i^2}.$$

Thus for b to be the BLUE estimator,

$$b = \Sigma a_i Y_i$$

$$= \frac{\Sigma x_i(y_i + \bar{Y})}{\Sigma x_i^2}$$

$$= \frac{\Sigma x_i y_i}{\Sigma x_i^2}, \quad \text{since } \Sigma x_i = 0,$$

and this is precisely the OLS estimator.

2.7. A similar method can be used to prove that the OLS estimator $\hat{\alpha}$ is the BLUE of α.

Let the BLUE be
$$k = \Sigma a_i Y_i$$

and therefore
$$E(k) = \Sigma a_i(\alpha + \beta X_i)$$
$$= \alpha\Sigma a_i + \beta\Sigma a_i X_i.$$

For $E(k) = \alpha$, we thus require

(a) $$\Sigma a_i = 1$$

(b) $$\Sigma a_i X_i = 0.$$

The Langrangean is

$$\mathcal{L} = \Sigma a_i^2 - \lambda_1(\Sigma a_i - 1) - \lambda_2 \Sigma a_i X_i,$$

and

$$\frac{\partial \mathcal{L}}{\partial a_i} = 2a_i - \lambda_1 - \lambda_2 X_i = 0,$$

from which

$$a_i = \frac{1}{2}\left(\lambda_1 + \lambda_2 X_i\right).$$

Substituting in the two constraints,

(a)
$$\frac{n\lambda_1}{2} + \frac{\lambda_2}{2} \Sigma X_i = 1$$

(b)
$$\lambda_1 \Sigma X_i + \lambda_2 \Sigma X_i^2 = 0$$

from which
$$\lambda_1 = \frac{2\Sigma X_i^2}{n\Sigma x_i^2}$$

and
$$\lambda_2 = -\frac{2\Sigma X_i}{n\Sigma x_i^2}$$

Thus
$$a_i = \frac{\Sigma X_i^2}{n\Sigma x_i^2} - \frac{X_i \Sigma X_i}{n\Sigma x_i^2}$$

and
$$k = \Sigma a_i Y_i$$

$$= \frac{\Sigma Y_i \Sigma X_i^2}{n\Sigma x_i^2} - \frac{\Sigma X_i Y_i \Sigma X_i}{n\Sigma x_i^2}$$

$$= \overline{Y} \frac{\Sigma X_i^2}{\Sigma x_i^2} - \overline{X} \frac{\Sigma X_i Y_i}{\Sigma x_i^2}$$

$$= \overline{Y} \frac{(\Sigma x_i^2 + nX^2)}{\Sigma x_i^2} - \overline{X} \frac{(\Sigma x_i y_i + n\overline{XY})}{\Sigma x_i^2}$$

$$= \overline{Y} - \beta\overline{X},$$

which is again the OLS estimator.

2.8. The variances of $\hat{\beta}$ and $\hat{\alpha}$ were shown above to be

$$\frac{\sigma^2}{\Sigma x_i^2} \quad \text{and} \quad \sigma^2\left(\frac{\overline{X}^2}{\Sigma x_i^2} + \frac{1}{n}\right)$$

respectively. However, σ^2, the variance of the true disturbances, is itself unknown and must be estimated on the basis of the data sample. Once the OLS line has been fitted, the residuals $(Y_i - \hat{Y}_i)$ or $(Y_i - \hat{\alpha} - \hat{\beta}X_i)$ can be computed, and an estimate of σ^2 based on the sum of these squared residuals:

$$e_i = Y_i - \hat{Y}_i$$

$$= y_i - \hat{y}_i$$

$$= \beta x_i + (u_i - \bar{u}) - \hat{\beta} x_i$$

$$= -(\hat{\beta} - \beta) x_i + (u_i - \bar{u}).$$

Thus $\qquad e_i^2 = (\hat{\beta} - \beta)^2 x_i^2 + (u_i - \bar{u})^2 - 2(\hat{\beta} - \beta)x_i(u_i - \bar{u})$

and $\qquad \Sigma e_i^2 = (\hat{\beta} - \beta)^2 \Sigma x_i^2 + \Sigma(u_i - \bar{u})^2 - 2(\hat{\beta} - \beta)\Sigma x_i(u_i - \bar{u}).$

Taking expectations of each term in turn:

$$E\{(\hat{\beta} - \beta)^2 \Sigma x_i^2\} = \text{var}\,(\hat{\beta})\,\Sigma x_i^2 = \sigma^2.$$

$$E\{\Sigma(u_i - \bar{u})^2\} = E\{\Sigma u_i^2 - 2\bar{u}\Sigma u_i + n\bar{u}^2\}$$

$$= E\{\Sigma u_i^2 - \frac{1}{n}(\Sigma u_i)^2\}$$

$$= n\sigma^2 - \sigma^2$$

since $\qquad E(\Sigma u_i)^2 = E(\Sigma u_i^2 + 2\Sigma u_i u_j),\ i < j.$

$$E\{-2(\hat{\beta} - \beta)\Sigma x_i(u_i - \bar{u})\} = -2E\left[\frac{\Sigma x_i u_i}{\Sigma x_i^2}(\Sigma x_i u_i - \bar{u}\Sigma x_i)\right]$$

$$= -2\sigma^2$$

since $\qquad E(u_i u_j) = 0,\ i \neq j,\quad \text{and}\quad \Sigma x_i = 0.$

Thus $\qquad E(\Sigma e_i^2) = \sigma^2 + n\sigma^2 - \sigma^2 - 2\sigma^2$

$$= \sigma^2(n - 2).$$

It follows that $\Sigma e_i^2/(n - 2)$ is an unbiased estimator of σ^2.

The formulae for computing $\text{var}\,(\hat{\alpha})$ and $\text{var}\,(\hat{\beta})$ are thus

$$\text{var}\,(\hat{\alpha}) = \frac{1}{n - 2}\,\Sigma e_i^2\left(\frac{\bar{X}^2}{\Sigma x_i^2} + \frac{1}{n}\right)$$

and $\qquad \text{var}\,(\hat{\beta}) = \frac{\Sigma e_i^2}{(n - 2)\Sigma x_i^2}.$

2.9. The least squares line can be written

$$y_i = \hat{y}_i + e_i.$$

Squaring and summing,

$$\Sigma y_i^2 = \Sigma \hat{y}_i^2 + \Sigma e_i^2 + 2\Sigma \hat{y}_i e_i.$$

But
$$\Sigma \hat{y}_i e_i = \hat{\beta}\Sigma x_i(y_i - \hat{\beta}x_i)$$
$$= \hat{\beta}^2\Sigma x_i^2 - \hat{\beta}^2\Sigma x_i^2 = 0.$$

Thus
$$\Sigma y_i^2 = \Sigma \hat{y}_i^2 + \Sigma e_i^2,$$

the total variation in Y_i about its mean value can be regarded as the sum of the variation 'explained' by the regression line, $\Sigma \hat{y}_i^2$, and the unexplained variation Σe_i^2.

Now
$$\frac{\Sigma \hat{y}_i^2}{\Sigma y_i^2} = \hat{\beta}^2 \frac{\Sigma x_i^2}{\Sigma y_i^2}$$

$$= \frac{(\Sigma x_i y_i)^2}{(\Sigma x_i^2)^2} \cdot \frac{\Sigma x_i^2}{\Sigma y_i^2}$$

$$= \frac{(\Sigma x_i y_i)^2}{\Sigma x_i^2 \Sigma y_i^2}$$

$$= r^2$$

where $r = \Sigma x_i y_i / (\sqrt{\Sigma x_i^2}\sqrt{\Sigma y_i^2})$, the correlation coefficient between X and Y. Thus r^2 provides a measure of the total variation in Y 'explained' by the regression line, $\Sigma \hat{y}^2/\Sigma y^2$.

A slightly different way of looking at r^2 is to regard it as the square of the correlation coefficient between y and $\hat{y}$ rather than between x and y. This would be:

$$\frac{(\Sigma y\hat{y})^2}{\Sigma y^2 \Sigma \hat{y}^2} = \frac{\{\Sigma(\hat{y} + e)\hat{y}\}^2}{\Sigma y^2 \Sigma \hat{y}^2}$$

$$= \frac{\{\Sigma(\hat{y}^2 + e\hat{y})\}^2}{\Sigma y^2 \Sigma \hat{y}^2}.$$

But we already know that $\Sigma e\hat{y} = 0$, and so this reduces to $\Sigma \hat{y}^2/\Sigma y^2$, the ratio of 'explained' to total variation.

Thus
$$r^2 = \frac{(\Sigma xy)^2}{\Sigma x^2 \Sigma y^2}$$

$$= \frac{\Sigma \hat{y}^2}{\Sigma y^2}$$

$$= 1 - \frac{\Sigma e^2}{\Sigma y^2}.$$

Further reading

J. Johnston, *Econometric methods* (2nd. edn), Chapter 2. McGraw-Hill, New York (1972).
J. Kmenta, *Elements of econometrics*, Chapter 7. Macmillan, New York (1971).
    A more advanced treatment is to be found in:
E. Malinvaud, *Statistical methods of econometrics* (2nd edn), Chapter 3. North-Holland, Amsterdam (1970).

Multiple regression and correlation

3.1. The multiple linear regression model results from the proposition that changes in one variable are a linear function of changes in several other variables:

$$Y_i = \alpha + \beta_1 X_{1i} + \beta_2 X_{2i} + \ldots + u_i$$

in which the dependent variable Y is related to the independent variables $X_1, X_2 \ldots$ etc., and to a disturbance u.

Most aspects of multiple regression analysis can be described in terms of a relationship with two independent variables without the algebra becoming so complex that matrix notation is a *sine qua non*. We shall thus assume the model

$$Y_i = \alpha + \beta_1 X_{1i} + \beta_2 X_{2i} + u_i$$

with the fitted line

$$\hat{Y}_i = \hat{\alpha} + \hat{\beta}_1 X_{1i} + \hat{\beta}_2 X_{2i}.$$

Applying the least squares criterion, we wish to choose $\hat{\alpha}, \hat{\beta}_1$, and $\hat{\beta}_2$ so as to minimize

$$S = \Sigma e_i^2 = \Sigma(Y_i - \hat{Y}_i)^2$$
$$= \Sigma(Y_i - \hat{\alpha} - \hat{\beta}_1 X_{1i} - \hat{\beta}_2 X_{2i})^2.$$

Differentiating partially with respect to $\hat{\alpha}, \hat{\beta}_1$, and $\hat{\beta}_2$, and setting each derivative equal to zero:

$$\frac{\partial S}{\partial \hat{\alpha}} = -2\Sigma(Y_i - \hat{\alpha} - \hat{\beta}_1 X_{1i} - \hat{\beta}_2 X_{2i}) = 0,$$

$$\frac{\partial S}{\partial \hat{\beta}_1} = -2\Sigma X_{1i}(Y_i - \hat{\alpha} - \hat{\beta}_1 X_{1i} - \hat{\beta}_2 X_{2i}) = 0,$$

$$\frac{\partial S}{\partial \hat{\beta}_2} = -2\Sigma X_{2i}(Y_i - \hat{\alpha} - \hat{\beta}_1 X_{1i} - \hat{\beta}_2 X_{2i}) = 0.$$

On rearrangement, these give the three normal equations:

$$\Sigma Y_i = n\hat{\alpha} + \hat{\beta}_1 \Sigma X_{1i} + \hat{\beta}_2 \Sigma X_{2i},$$

$$\Sigma Y_i X_{1i} = \hat{\alpha}\Sigma X_{1i} + \hat{\beta}_1 \Sigma X_{1i}^2 + \hat{\beta}_2 \Sigma X_{1i}X_{2i},$$

$$\Sigma Y_i X_{2i} = \hat{\alpha}\Sigma X_{2i} + \hat{\beta}_1 \Sigma X_{1i}X_{2i} + \hat{\beta}_2 \Sigma X_{2i}^2.$$

We thus have three equations to solve for the three unknowns $\hat{\alpha}, \hat{\beta}_1$, and $\hat{\beta}_2$ in terms of sums of squares and cross-products obtainable from the data. (It will be seen that the normal equations are easily generalized to the case of k independent variables. The jth normal equation will be (omitting the observation subscript):

$$\Sigma YX_j = \hat{\alpha}\Sigma X_j + \hat{\beta}_1\Sigma X_1 X_j + \hat{\beta}_2\Sigma X_2 X_j + \ldots + \hat{\beta}_j\Sigma X_j^2 + \ldots + \hat{\beta}_k\Sigma X_k X_j.$$

Together with the first normal equation

$$\Sigma Y = n\hat{\alpha} + \hat{\beta}_1\Sigma X_1 + \ldots + \hat{\beta}_j\Sigma X_j + \ldots + \hat{\beta}_k\Sigma X_k$$

this will give $(k + 1)$ normal equations to solve for the $(k + 1)$ coefficients.)

Alternatively, we may adopt the device used in the case of simple regression by noting that the first normal equation can be written

$$\overline{Y} = \hat{\alpha} + \hat{\beta}_1\overline{X}_1 + \hat{\beta}_2\overline{X}_2$$

and thus the two remaining equations can be written (dropping the observation i subscript for clarity):

$$\Sigma yx_1 = \hat{\beta}_1\Sigma x_1^2 + \hat{\beta}_2\Sigma x_1 x_2 \tag{3.1}$$

$$\Sigma yx_2 = \hat{\beta}_1\Sigma x_1 x_2 + \hat{\beta}_2\Sigma x_2^2, \tag{3.2}$$

where lower-case letters for variables denote deviations from means.

Again, these may be solved simultaneously for $\hat{\beta}_1$ and $\hat{\beta}_2$, $\hat{\alpha}$ being obtained as

$$\hat{\alpha} = \overline{Y} - \hat{\beta}_1\overline{X}_1 - \hat{\beta}_2\overline{X}_2,$$

or they may be solved directly, for from eqn (3.2)

$$\hat{\beta}_2 = \frac{\Sigma yx_2 - \hat{\beta}_1\Sigma x_1 x_2}{\Sigma x_2^2}$$

and on substitution in eqn (3.1):

$$\Sigma yx_1 = \hat{\beta}_1\Sigma x_1^2 + \frac{(\Sigma yx_2 - \hat{\beta}_1\Sigma x_1 x_2)}{\Sigma x_2^2}\Sigma x_1 x_2$$

or $$\hat{\beta}_1 = \frac{\Sigma yx_1\Sigma x_2^2 - \Sigma yx_2\Sigma x_1 x_2}{\Sigma x_1^2\Sigma x_2^2 - (\Sigma x_1 x_2)^2}. \tag{3.3}$$

Similarly, $$\hat{\beta}_2 = \frac{\Sigma yx_2\Sigma x_1^2 - \Sigma yx_1\Sigma x_1 x_2}{\Sigma x_1^2\Sigma x_2^2 - (\Sigma x_1 x_2)^2}. \tag{3.4}$$

3.2. In order to investigate the econometric properties of these estimators, we need to establish relationships between them and the true but unknown parameters α, β_1, and β_2. As before, this is done by substituting the true relationship for Y_i (or y_i) in the estimating formulae. The algebra is cumbersome, though straightforward, but it is worth following through since it will be used persistently in the remainder of this book to show the econometric consequences of relaxing the assumptions which are made in OLS estimation.

Turning first to $\hat{\beta}_1$, we substitute

$$y = \beta_1 x_1 + \beta_2 x_2 + (u - \bar{u})$$

in eqn. (3.3) to obtain

$$\hat{\beta}_1 = \frac{\Sigma x_1\{\beta_1 x_1 + \beta_2 x_2 + (u - \bar{u})\}\Sigma x_2^2 - \Sigma x_2\{\beta_1 x_1 + \beta_2 x_2 + (u - \bar{u})\}\Sigma x_1 x_2}{\Sigma x_1^2 \Sigma x_2^2 - (\Sigma x_1 x_2)^2}$$

$$= \frac{\beta_1\{\Sigma x_1^2 \Sigma x_2^2 - (\Sigma x_1 x_2)^2\} + \Sigma(u - \bar{u})x_1 \Sigma x_2^2 - \Sigma(u - \bar{u})x_2 \Sigma x_1 x_2}{D}$$

(where $\quad D = \Sigma x_1^2 \Sigma x_2^2 - (\Sigma x_1 x_2)^2$)

$$= \beta_1 + \frac{\Sigma(u - \bar{u})x_1 \Sigma x_2^2 - \Sigma(u - \bar{u})x_2 \Sigma x_1 x_2}{D}$$

Taking expectations,

$$E(\hat{\beta}_1) = \beta_1 + E\left[\frac{\Sigma u x_1 \Sigma x_2^2 - \bar{u}\Sigma x_1 \Sigma x_2^2 - \Sigma u x_2 \Sigma x_1 x_2 + \bar{u}\Sigma x_2 \Sigma x_1 x_2}{D}\right]$$

$$= \beta_1,$$

since $E(\Sigma u x_1) = \Sigma x_1 E(u) = 0$ (since $E(u) = 0$), $E(\Sigma u x_2) = 0$ similarly, and $\Sigma x_1 = \Sigma x_2 = 0$. Thus $\hat{\beta}_1$ is an unbiased estimator of β_1.

For the variance of $\hat{\beta}_1$, we have

$$\text{var}(\hat{\beta}_1) = E[\hat{\beta}_1 - E(\hat{\beta}_1)]^2$$

$$= E(\hat{\beta}_1 - \beta_1)^2, \quad \text{since } E(\hat{\beta}_1) = \beta_1,$$

$$= E\left[\frac{\Sigma x_1(u - \bar{u})\Sigma x_2^2 - \Sigma x_2(u - \bar{u})\Sigma x_1 x_2}{D}\right]^2$$

$$= \frac{1}{D^2} E[\{\Sigma x_1(u - \bar{u})\}^2(\Sigma x_2^2)^2 + \{\Sigma x_2(u - \bar{u})\}^2(\Sigma x_1 x_2)^2 - \\ - 2\Sigma x_1(u - \bar{u})\Sigma x_2(u - \bar{u})\Sigma x_2^2 \Sigma x_1 x_2]$$

$$= \frac{1}{D^2} E\{(\Sigma x_2^2)^2(\Sigma x_1 u - \bar{u}\Sigma x_1)^2 + (\Sigma x_1 x_2)^2(\Sigma x_2 u - \bar{u}\Sigma x_2)^2 - \\ - 2(\Sigma x_1 u - \bar{u}\Sigma x_1)(\Sigma x_2 u - \bar{u}\Sigma x_2)\Sigma x_2^2 \Sigma x_1 x_2\}$$

$$= \frac{1}{D^2} \{(\Sigma x_2^2)^2 \sigma^2 \Sigma x_1^2 + (\Sigma x_1 x_2)^2 \sigma^2 \Sigma x_2^2 - 2\sigma^2 \Sigma x_1 x_2 \Sigma x_2^2 \Sigma x_1 x_2\}$$

since $\quad \Sigma x_1 = \Sigma x_2 = 0, \text{ and } E(u_i u_j) = \sigma^2, \ i = j$

$$= 0, \quad i \neq j.$$

Thus
$$\text{var}(\hat{\beta}_1) = \frac{\sigma^2 \Sigma x_2^2 \{\Sigma x_1^2 \Sigma x_2^2 - (\Sigma x_1 x_2)^2\}}{D^2}$$

$$= \frac{\sigma^2 \Sigma x_2^2}{D}$$

$$= \frac{\sigma^2 \Sigma x_2^2}{\Sigma x_1^2 \Sigma x_2^2 - (\Sigma x_1 x_2)^2} \cdot$$

Similarly,
$$\text{var}(\hat{\beta}_2) = \frac{\sigma^2 \Sigma x_1^2}{\Sigma x_1^2 \Sigma x_2^2 - (\Sigma x_1 x_2)^2} \cdot$$

For the covariance of $\hat{\beta}_1$ and $\hat{\beta}_2$, we have

$$\text{covar}(\hat{\beta}_1, \hat{\beta}_2) = E\{\hat{\beta}_1 - E(\hat{\beta}_1)\}\{\hat{\beta}_2 - E(\hat{\beta}_2)\}$$

$$= E(\hat{\beta}_1 - \beta_1)(\hat{\beta}_2 - \beta_2)$$

$$= \frac{1}{D^2} E\{\Sigma x_1(u - \bar{u})\Sigma x_2^2 - \Sigma x_2(u - \bar{u})\Sigma x_1 x_2\}\{\Sigma x_2(u - \bar{u})\Sigma x_1^2 -$$
$$- \Sigma x_1(u - \bar{u})\Sigma x_1 x_2\}$$

$$= \frac{1}{D^2} E\{\Sigma x_2^2(\Sigma x_1 u - \bar{u}\Sigma x_1) - \Sigma x_1 x_2(\Sigma x_2 u - \bar{u}\Sigma x_2)\}\{\Sigma x_1^2(\Sigma x_2 u - \bar{u}\Sigma x_2) -$$
$$- \Sigma x_1 x_2(\Sigma x_1 u - \bar{u}\Sigma x_1)\}$$

$$= \frac{1}{D^2} \{\sigma^2 \Sigma x_1^2 \Sigma x_2^2 \Sigma x_1 x_2 - \sigma^2 \Sigma x_1^2 \Sigma x_2^2 \Sigma x_1 x_2 -$$
$$- \sigma^2 \Sigma x_1^2 \Sigma x_2^2 \Sigma x_1 x_2 + \sigma^2 (\Sigma x_1 x_2)^3\}$$

$$= \frac{1}{D^2} \sigma^2 \Sigma x_1 x_2 \{(\Sigma x_1 x_2)^2 - \Sigma x_1^2 \Sigma x_2^2\}$$

$$= \frac{-\sigma^2 \Sigma x_1 x_2}{\Sigma x_1^2 \Sigma x_2^2 - (\Sigma x_1 x_2)^2} \cdot$$

Using the same method as in §2.4 above, it is easily shown that

$$\hat{\alpha} = \alpha - (\hat{\beta}_1 - \beta_1)\bar{X}_1 - (\hat{\beta}_2 - \beta_2)\bar{X}_2 + \frac{1}{n}\Sigma u$$

from which

$$\text{var}(\hat{\alpha}) = \bar{X}_1^2 \text{var}(\hat{\beta}_1) + \bar{X}_2^2 \text{var}(\hat{\beta}_2) + 2\bar{X}_1\bar{X}_2 \text{covar}(\hat{\beta}_1, \hat{\beta}_2) + \frac{\sigma^2}{n}$$

3.3. Again, these formulae (and the remaining ones for $\text{covar}(\hat{\alpha}, \hat{\beta}_1)$ and $\text{covar}(\hat{\alpha}, \hat{\beta}_2)$) are all expressed in terms of σ^2 which is itself unknown. As before, we take the sum of squares of the residuals from the fitted regression and investigate its properties as an estimator of σ^2:

$$e_i = Y_i - \hat{\alpha} - \hat{\beta}_1 X_{1i} - \hat{\beta}_2 X_{2i}$$

$$= y_i - \hat{\beta}_1 x_{1i} - \hat{\beta}_2 x_{2i}.$$

Squaring and summing, after substituting $\beta_1 x_{1i} + \beta_2 x_{2i} + (u_i - \bar{u})$ for y_i:

$$\Sigma e^2 = \Sigma\{-(\hat{\beta}_1 - \beta_1)x_1 - (\hat{\beta}_2 - \beta_2)x_2 + (u - \bar{u})\}^2$$

(dropping the i subscript), and

$$E(\Sigma e^2) = \Sigma x_1^2 \operatorname{var}(\hat{\beta}_1) + \Sigma x_2^2 \operatorname{var}(\hat{\beta}_2) + 2 \operatorname{covar}(\hat{\beta}_1, \hat{\beta}_2)\Sigma x_1 x_2 - $$
$$- 2E(\hat{\beta}_1 - \beta_1)\Sigma x_1(u - \bar{u}) - 2E(\hat{\beta}_2 - \beta_2)\Sigma x_2(u - \bar{u}) + E\Sigma(u - \bar{u})^2.$$

Taking each of these terms in turn:

$$\Sigma x_1^2 \operatorname{var}(\hat{\beta}_1) = (1/D)\sigma^2 \Sigma x_1^2 \Sigma x_2^2$$

$$\Sigma x_2^2 \operatorname{var}(\hat{\beta}_2) = (1/D)\sigma^2 \Sigma x_1^2 \Sigma x_2^2$$

$$2 \operatorname{covar}(\hat{\beta}_1, \hat{\beta}_2)\Sigma x_1 x_2 = (-2/D)\sigma^2(\Sigma x_1 x_2)^2$$

$$E(\hat{\beta}_1 - \beta_1)\Sigma x_1(u - u) = (1/D)E[\{\Sigma x_2^2 \Sigma x_1(u - \bar{u}) - \Sigma x_1 x_2 \Sigma x_2(u - \bar{u})\}\Sigma x_1(u - \bar{u})$$
$$= (1/D)\{\sigma^2 \Sigma x_1^2 \Sigma x_2^2 - \sigma^2(\Sigma x_1 x_2)^2\}$$
$$= \sigma^2$$

and, similarly, $\qquad E(\hat{\beta}_2 - \beta_2)\Sigma X_2(u - \bar{u}) = \sigma^2$

Finally, $\qquad E\Sigma(u - \bar{u})^2 = (n - 1)\sigma^2,$

and thus $\qquad E(\Sigma e^2) = 2\sigma^2 - 2\sigma^2 - 2\sigma^2 + (n - 1)\sigma^2$
$$= (n - 3)\sigma^2.$$

Hence $\Sigma e^2/(n - 3)$ is an unbiased estimator of σ^2.

It will readily be seen that if there are $(k + 1)$ regression coefficients to be estimated (i.e. the regression equation has a constant plus k independent variables) then

$$s^2 = \frac{1}{n - k - 1} \Sigma e^2$$

is the unbiased estimator of σ^2. The number $(n - k - 1)$ is often referred to as the number of degrees of freedom of the regression.

3.4. As in the case of simple regression, the proof that the least squares estimators of the coefficients are BLUE is straightforward, but a little tedious. We shall sketch here the proof for $\hat{\beta}_1$; parallel proofs can be conducted for $\hat{\alpha}$ and $\hat{\beta}_2$.

The general linear estimator of β_1 is

$$b_1 = \Sigma a_i Y_i$$
$$= \Sigma a_i(\alpha + \beta_1 X_{1i} + \beta_2 X_{2i} + u_i)$$

and $\qquad E(b_1) = \alpha\Sigma a_i + \beta_1\Sigma a_i X_{1i} + \beta_2\Sigma a_i X_{2i},$

which is unbiased if

(a) $$\Sigma a_i = 0$$

(b) $$\Sigma a_i X_{1i} = 1$$

(c) $$\Sigma a_i X_{2i} = 0.$$

Since $$\mathrm{var}(b) = \mathrm{var}(\Sigma a_i Y_i) = E(\Sigma a_i Y_i)^2 = \sigma^2 \Sigma a_i^2,$$

to find the minimum variance unbiased estimator we have to minimize Σa_i^2 subject to the constraints (a)–(c). The Langrangean is thus

$$\mathcal{L} = \Sigma a_i^2 - \lambda_1 \Sigma a_i - \lambda_2 (\Sigma a_i X_{1i} - 1) - \lambda_3 \Sigma a_i X_{2i}.$$

This gives

$$\frac{\partial \mathcal{L}}{\partial a_i} = 2a_i - \lambda_1 - \lambda_2 X_{1i} - \lambda_3 X_{2i} = 0.$$

On substitution in the constraints (a) – (c):

$$n\lambda_1 + \lambda_2 \Sigma X_1 + \lambda_3 \Sigma X_2 = 0,$$

$$\lambda_1 \Sigma X_1 + \lambda_2 \Sigma X_1^2 + \lambda_3 \Sigma X_1 X_2 = 2,$$

$$\lambda_1 \Sigma X_2 + \lambda_2 \Sigma X_1 X_2 + \lambda_3 \Sigma X_2^2 = 0,$$

(dropping the i subscript), and these solve to give

$$\lambda_1 = \frac{2(-\bar{X}_1 \Sigma x_2^2 + \bar{X}_2 \Sigma x_1 x_2)}{D}$$

$$\lambda_2 = \frac{2\Sigma x_2^2}{D}$$

$$\lambda_3 = -\frac{2\Sigma x_1 x_2}{D}.$$

Hence

$$a = \frac{1}{2}(\lambda_1 + \lambda_2 X_1 + \lambda_3 X_2)$$

$$= \frac{-\bar{X}_1 \Sigma x_2^2 + \bar{X}_2 \Sigma x_1 x_2 + X_1 \Sigma x_2^2 - X_2 \Sigma x_1 x_2}{D}$$

$$= \frac{x_1 \Sigma x_2^2 - x_2 \Sigma x_1 x_2}{D}$$

Then $b_1 = \Sigma a Y = \Sigma a(y + \bar{Y}) = \Sigma ay$ (since $\Sigma a = 0$)

$$= \frac{\Sigma x_1 y \Sigma x_2^2 - \Sigma x_2 y \Sigma x_1 x_2}{D}$$

which is precisely the OLS estimator.

3.5. We may define a coefficient of multiple correlation analogous to the simple correlation coefficient described in §2.9 above.

The regression line is

$$\hat{y} = \hat{\beta}_1 x_1 + \hat{\beta}_2 x_2.$$

Thus, since

$$y = \hat{y} + e,$$

$$\Sigma y^2 = \Sigma \hat{y}^2 + \Sigma e^2 + 2\Sigma \hat{y} e.$$

But

$$\Sigma \hat{y} e = \Sigma(\hat{\beta}_1 x_1 + \hat{\beta}_2 x_2)(y - \hat{\beta}_1 x_1 - \hat{\beta}_2 x_2)$$

$$= \hat{\beta}_1 \Sigma x_1 y + \hat{\beta}_2 \Sigma x_2 y - \hat{\beta}_1^2 \Sigma x_1^2 - \hat{\beta}_2^2 \Sigma x_2^2 - 2\hat{\beta}_1 \hat{\beta}_2 \Sigma x_1 x_2.$$

Furthermore, from the normal equations,

$$\Sigma x_1 y = \hat{\beta}_1 \Sigma x_1^2 + \hat{\beta}_2 \Sigma x_1 x_2$$

and thus

$$\hat{\beta}_1 \Sigma x_1 y = \hat{\beta}_1^2 \Sigma x_1^2 + \hat{\beta}_1 \hat{\beta}_2 \Sigma x_1 x_2.$$

Similarly

$$\hat{\beta}_2 \Sigma x_2 y = \hat{\beta}_1 \hat{\beta}_2 \Sigma x_1 x_2 + \hat{\beta}_2^2 \Sigma x_1^2.$$

Thus

$$\Sigma \hat{y} e = 0.$$

Hence, as before,

$$\Sigma \hat{y}^2 = \Sigma \hat{y}^2 + \Sigma e^2,$$

the total variation of Y about its mean is the sum of the explained variation, $\Sigma \hat{y}^2$, and the variation of the residual, Σe^2. Again the square of the correlation coefficient (written as R^2 to denote multiple rather than simple correlation) is

$$R^2 = \frac{\Sigma \hat{y}^2}{\Sigma y^2} = 1 - \frac{\Sigma e^2}{\Sigma y^2}.$$

Note that since

$$\Sigma y \hat{y} = \Sigma(\hat{y} + e)\hat{y} = \Sigma \hat{y}^2,$$

and

$$\hat{y} = \hat{\beta}_1 x_1 + \hat{\beta}_2 x_2,$$

whence

$$\Sigma y \hat{y} = \hat{\beta}_1 \Sigma x_1 y + \hat{\beta}_2 \Sigma x_2 y,$$

a convenient way of computing R^2 is as

$$R^2 = \frac{\hat{\beta}_1 \Sigma x_1 y + \hat{\beta}_2 \Sigma x_2 y}{\Sigma y^2}$$

or, in general,

$$R^2 = \frac{\sum_k (\hat{\beta}_k \sum_i x_{ki} y_i)}{\sum_i y_i^2}.$$

3.6. It was mentioned above (§1.4) that one way of looking at multiple regression analysis was to see it as a way of 'correcting' the correlations between Y

and each of the Xs for the correlation between the Xs themselves. This is easily seen for the three variable cases, for

$$\hat{\beta}_1 = \frac{\Sigma yx_1 \Sigma x_2^2 - \Sigma yx_2 \Sigma x_1 x_2}{\Sigma x_1^2 \Sigma x_2^2 - (\Sigma x_1 x_2)^2}$$

and the simple correlation coefficient between Y and X_1 can be written

$$r_{y1} = \frac{\Sigma yx_1}{\sqrt{\Sigma y^2} \sqrt{\Sigma x_1^2}}$$

and similarly for the other simple correlation coefficients r_{y2} and r_{12}. Thus

$$\hat{\beta}_1 = \frac{(r_{y1}\sqrt{\Sigma y^2}\sqrt{\Sigma x_1^2})\,\Sigma x_2^2 - (r_{y2}\sqrt{\Sigma y^2}\sqrt{\Sigma x_2^2})r_{12}\sqrt{\Sigma x_1^2}\sqrt{\Sigma x_2^2}}{\Sigma x_1^2 \Sigma x_2^2 - r_{12}^2 \Sigma x_1^2 \Sigma x_2^2}$$

$$= \frac{r_{y1} - r_{y2}\cdot r_{12}}{1 - r_{12}^2} \cdot \frac{s_y}{s_1} \tag{3.5}$$

where s_y, the standard deviation of Y, is $\sqrt{(\Sigma y^2/n)}$, etc.

This may be compared with the corresponding expression for $\hat{\beta}_1$ in the simple regression of Y on X_1,

$$\hat{\beta}_1 = r_{y1} \frac{s_y}{s_1}$$

which is exactly eqn (3.5) in the case where $r_{12} = 0$, the correlation between X_1 and X_2, is zero.

3.7. The multiple correlation coefficient R^2 is often used to compare the goodness of fit of one equation with that of another fitted to the same data. On the face of things, if equation A has a higher R^2 than equation B (i.e. A 'explains' more of the variation in Y than B) then equation A is 'better' (subject, of course, to a multitude of provisos, not least of which will be economic common sense). But the value of R^2 can be improved at will simply by including more variables; in the limit, with the number of variables equal (with the constant) to the number of observations, R^2 must be equal to one. If the 'better' equation A contains more independent variables than equation B, the R^2s are not, on this account, on the same footing, and simply comparing them may be misleading. The obvious answer is to 'correct' R^2 for the number of degrees of freedom of the regression. The resulting quantity is denoted by $\bar{R}^2$ and is given by

$$\bar{R}^2 = 1 - \text{var}(e)/\text{var}(y)$$

$$= 1 - \frac{\Sigma e^2/(n - k - 1)}{\Sigma y^2/(n - 1)}$$

(where n is the number of observations and k is the number of independent variables), compared with

$$R^2 = 1 - (\Sigma e^2 / \Sigma y^2).$$

The relationship between the two is clear:

$$\bar{R}^2 = 1 - \frac{(n-1)}{(n-k-1)} \frac{\Sigma e^2}{\Sigma y^2}$$

$$= 1 - \frac{(n-1)}{(n-k-1)} (1 - R^2).$$

Further reading

J. Johnston, *Econometric methods* (2nd. edn.), Chapter 5. McGraw-Hill, New York (1972).
A. S. Goldberger, *Econometric theory*, Chapter IV. Wiley, New York (1964).
E. Malinvaud, *Statistical methods of econometrics* (2nd. edn.), Chapter 6. North-Holland, Amsterdam (1970).

<table>
<tr><td>

4

</td><td>

Hypothesis testing and prediction

</td></tr>
</table>

4.1. So far, we have shown how it is possible to obtain estimates of the parameters of a linear model by the method of least squares. Under certain assumptions about the error term in the assumed true model, we have seen that each of these estimates can be thought of as one drawing from a distribution centred on the true value of the parameter, and whose variance can be estimated. Formally, for the simple regression case, if the true relationship is

$$Y_i = \alpha + \beta X_i + u_i$$

where

$$E(u_i) = 0$$

$$E(u_i u_j) = \sigma^2, \ i = j$$

$$= 0, \ i \neq j$$

then

$$E(\hat{\beta}) = \beta$$

and   estimated $var(\hat{\beta}) = \dfrac{s^2}{\Sigma x_i^2} = \dfrac{1}{n-2} \cdot \dfrac{\Sigma(y_i - \hat{y})^2}{\Sigma x_i^2}$

Two kinds of use can be made of this information. First, we may wish to use it in order to make inferences about the true parameter, and in particular to lend support to, or cast doubt on, some hypothesis which we had already formulated about the true value of the parameter. For example, suppose we have data on the income and consumption of a number of families whose income is relatively low and, by regression analysis, estimate that the marginal propensity to consume is 0·9. Then we may wish to ask whether the evidence is consistent with the view that the true marginal propensity is 1 − that this group does not save at all. In effect, we should be asking whether our sample could reasonably be thought to have been drawn from a population with a zero marginal savings propensity on average.

Secondly, we may have no hypothesis which we wish to test directly, but we may want to predict future behaviour. If we have estimated a consumption function in national aggregate terms, we may use it to predict how much consumption would rise if national income were to rise by a given amount. But because our consumption function is only an estimate of the true consumption function, and because of the disturbance term in the true relationship, a degree of error will attach to such predictions. How big is the margin of error?

4.2. Although the variance of $\hat{\beta}$ is a measure of how 'spread out' the distribution of $\hat{\beta}$ is, the assumptions we have made so far do not allow us to make any inferences about the precise shape of the distribution. For example, each of the following distributions might have the same variance (Fig. 4.1). But they would have quite different implications for propositions such as 'there is a 5% chance, given β, that $\hat{\beta}$ could be greater than x'.

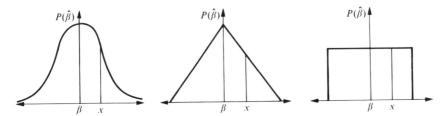

Fig. 4.1. Different distributions of an estimator

However, since $\hat{\beta}$ is a linear function of the Y_i and thus of the disturbance terms u_i, the distribution of $\hat{\beta}$ will depend on the distribution of the disturbances. It can be shown that if the disturbances are symmetrically distributed about zero and if the likelihood of a disturbance of a particular (absolute) size is inversely proportional to its size, then the disturbance term will be a drawing from a population which follows the normal distribution. (These two sentences are deliberately unrigorous. A description of the normal distribution and the justification of the assertion that the distribution of a random error term will conform to it will be found in any standard statistical text.) Although the 'shape' of the normal distribution is given, each particular distribution will differ according to the mean and variance in question. It is easy to reduce any normal distribution to the standard normal distribution which has zero mean, unit variance, and total area equal to one, and which has been tabulated. If X_i is normally distributed with mean μ and variance $\sigma^2(x)$, then

$$Z = \frac{X_i - \mu}{\sigma(x)}$$

will follow the standard normal distribution. It follows that since the mean of the distribution of the OLS estimator $\hat{\beta}$ is β and it has variance $\sigma^2(\hat{\beta})$, then

$$Z = \frac{\hat{\beta} - \beta}{\sigma(\hat{\beta})}$$

will follow the standard normal distribution.

Suppose that the hypothesis which we wish to test is that $\beta = 0$; the true value of β is zero. We obtain by simple regression analysis an estimate $\hat{\beta}$ which is not zero, and whose variance is $\sigma^2(\hat{\beta}) = \sigma^2/\Sigma x^2$ (for the moment, assume that σ^2, the variance of the disturbance term, is known). Form the standard normal variable

$$Z = \frac{\hat{\beta} - 0}{\sigma(\hat{\beta})} = \hat{\beta}/\sigma(\hat{\beta}).$$

Now if Z is 'large', the probability is that the hypothesis $\beta = 0$ can be rejected, for there will then be only a small chance that $\hat{\beta}$ would have come from a population whose true mean was zero. How large Z must be to qualify for rejection is a matter of choice. Suppose that we wish to tolerate only a 5% chance of wrongly rejecting the null hypothesis. Then the critical value of Z is such that only 5% of the area under the standard normal distribution is associated with higher values of Z. The hypothesis which will be accepted if the null hypothesis is rejected is simply that $\beta \neq 0$. This can be satisfied by values of β significantly greater *or significantly less* than zero; the test variable Z could be significantly positive or significantly negative. We are thus performing a *two-tailed* test; if there is to be only a 5% chance of wrongly rejecting the null hypothesis, this must mean a $2\frac{1}{2}\%$ chance of wrong rejection on the basis of a large positive value of Z and a $2\frac{1}{2}\%$ chance on the basis of a large negative Z.

Statistical tables generally give only half the distribution, since it is symmetrical; it will be seen that $Z_{0.025}$ (corresponding to 0·475 of the area) is 1·96. Thus if Z is greater than 1·96 or less than −1·96, the null hypothesis can be rejected at the 5% level of significance, or with 95% confidence.

Essentially the same reasoning can be inverted in order to derive what is known as a confidence interval. Given an estimated value $\hat{\beta}$, it follows that one can say with 95% confidence that the true value of β lies within 1·96 standard errors either way of $\hat{\beta}$. If this confidence interval contains zero, of course, the null hypothesis cannot be rejected at the 5% level of significance.

The null hypothesis need not be that $\beta = 0$, but that $\beta = \beta_0$ where β_0 is any value chosen *a priori*. The alternative hypothesis has so far been assumed to be $\beta \neq \beta_0$. Suppose, however, that the null hypothesis is $\beta \geqslant \beta_0$, the alternative hypothesis then being $\beta < \beta_0$. In this case, we shall wish to perform a *one-tail* test. In other words, we wish to run only a (say) 5% chance that β could be *less* than β_0. The critical value of Z is now $Z_{0.05} = 1·64$. Only if $(\hat{\beta} - \beta_0)/\sigma(\hat{\beta})$ is greater than 1·64 can we accept the hypothesis $\beta \geqslant \beta_0$ with 95% confidence.

4.3. So far, it has been assumed that σ^2, the variance of the disturbances, is known. In practice, it must be estimated on the basis of the residuals from the fitted equation. We have already seen that

$$s^2 = \frac{1}{n - k - 1} \cdot \Sigma e^2$$

is an unbiased estimator of σ^2, and this suggests replacing Z as a test statistic by

$$t = \frac{\hat{\beta} - \beta_0}{s(\hat{\beta})}$$

where $s(\hat{\beta}) = s/\sqrt{(\Sigma x^2)}$, the estimated standard error of $\hat{\beta}$. There is, however, a difficulty. In the expression for Z, $\sigma(\hat{\beta})$ is a fixed parameter based on the true standard deviation of the population of disturbances. In the expression for t, $s(\hat{\beta})$ is simply an estimate of $\sigma(\hat{\beta})$, so that instead of being a fixed parameter, it itself has a sampling distribution. The *t-statistic*, in consequence, does not follow the normal distribution but a distribution known as *Student's t*. Of course, as the sample size increases towards infinity, the variance of $s(\hat{\beta})$ decreases; $s(\hat{\beta})$ becomes more 'like' a parameter and the *t*-distribution approaches the normal distribution. But for small samples, the *t*-distribution, which is different for different sample sizes, is significantly different from the normal distribution. The point at which the two distributions become significantly different is, of course, a matter of judgement. For example when the number of degrees of freedom $(n - k - 1)$ is 30, $t_{0.025} = 2 \cdot 04$ while $Z_{0.025} = 1 \cdot 96$.

The *t*-distribution is, however, always symmetrical; with the proviso that the appropriate *t*-value depends on the number of degrees of freedom of the regression, the procedures for testing hypotheses and setting up confidence intervals are exactly as described in §4.2 above for the case of a normally-distributed variable.

4.4. Tests of hypotheses concerning two parameters follow straightforwardly. For example, consider the problem of testing the hypothesis $\beta_1 = \beta_2$, given OLS estimates $\hat{\beta}_1$ and $\hat{\beta}_2$. The hypothesis can be expressed as $(\beta_1 - \beta_2) = 0$, suggesting the test statistic

$$t = \frac{\hat{\beta}_1 - \hat{\beta}_2}{s(\hat{\beta}_1 - \hat{\beta}_2)}.$$

The only problem is to find the standard error of $(\hat{\beta}_1 - \hat{\beta}_2)$. The variance of $(\hat{\beta}_1 - \hat{\beta}_2)$ is

$$\mathrm{var}\,(\hat{\beta}_1 - \hat{\beta}_2) = E\{(\hat{\beta}_1 - \hat{\beta}_2) - E(\hat{\beta}_1 - \hat{\beta}_2)\}^2$$

$$= E\{(\hat{\beta}_1 - \hat{\beta}_2) - (\beta_1 - \beta_2)\}^2$$

(since $\hat{\beta}_1$ and $\hat{\beta}_2$ are unbiased estimates of β_1 and β_2)

$$= E\{(\hat{\beta}_1 - \beta_1)^2 + (\hat{\beta}_2 - \beta_2)^2 - 2(\hat{\beta}_1 - \beta_1)(\hat{\beta}_2 - \beta_2)\}$$

$$= \mathrm{var}\,(\hat{\beta}_1) + \mathrm{var}\,(\hat{\beta}_2) - 2\,\mathrm{covar}\,(\hat{\beta}_1, \hat{\beta}_2).$$

The terms of this expression are easily computed (see §3.2 above) and the square root of their sum is then $s(\hat{\beta}_1 - \hat{\beta}_2)$. The hypothesis is then tested in precisely the same way as in the case of the single parameter hypothesis $\beta = 0$. This will, of course, be a two-tailed test since the alternative to the null hypothesis $\beta_1 = \beta_2$ is simply $\beta_1 \neq \beta_2$. If the alternative hypothesis were $\beta_1 > \beta_2$ (or $\beta_1 < \beta_2$), a one-tail test would be appropriate.

4.5. A further distribution which is of some importance is the *F-distribution*. This is used in testing the significance of a regression equation as a whole, in effect as an alternative to R^2 or $\bar{R}^2$, but with the advantage that a significance level can be used.

We have already seen that

$$\Sigma y^2 = \Sigma \hat{y}^2 + \Sigma e^2,$$

that is, that the total sum of squares (Σy^2) consists of the sum of squares explained by the regression $(\Sigma \hat{y}^2)$ and the residual sum of squares (Σe^2). R^2 is the ratio of the explained to the total sum of squares, and can vary between zero and one. Alternatively, consider the ratio of the sum of squares explained by the regression to the residual sum of squares. This can vary between zero, when the regression equation explains none of the variance of Y, and infinity, when the whole of the variance of Y is explained.

Now it can be shown that, if allowance is made for the number of degrees of freedom in the estimation, the quantity

$$\frac{\Sigma \hat{y}^2/k}{\Sigma e^2/(n-k-1)}$$

follows what is known as the F-distribution, which is characterised by two separate degrees of freedom, k in the denominator and $(n-k-1)$ in the numerator, where as before n is the number of observations and k the number of independent variables.

The F—test may be used in two ways. First, it may be used to test the significance of the regression as a whole; if the value of the statistic is less than the chosen critical value, the null hypothesis that the regression as a whole is not significant (i.e. the null hypothesis that $\beta_1 = \beta_2 = \ldots = \beta_k = 0$) cannot be rejected. For example, if we have 20 observations and three independent variables together with a constant, so that $k = 3$, $(n-k-1) = 16$, then $F_{3,16}^{0.05} = 3 \cdot 24$ is the value of F, at the 5% level of significance, which must be exceeded if the null hypothesis is to be rejected.

The second use of the F-test for the regression as a whole is in judging between different regressions. Like $\bar{R}^2$, allowance is made for differences in the numbers of degrees of freedom in the equations, and the equation with the higher value of F can be regarded as the 'better' (statistically) of two alternative regressions.

4.6. As well as finding out how much of the total variation in Y is explained by the regression as a whole, we may be interested in discovering how much of the variation is explained by each of the independent variables in the regression, and in whether the increase in the explained variation obtained by including a variable is significant.

This latter aspect is clearly connected with the question of whether the regression coefficient of the variable is significantly different from zero. In fact, the square of the t—statistic is an F—statistic measuring the ratio of the variance of Y explained by the independent variable in question to the variance of the residual error. Thus for the jth explanatory variable X_j, with estimated regression coefficient $\hat{\beta}_j$ having an estimated standard error of s_j:

$$\hat{\beta}_j/s_j = t_j$$

and

$$t_j^2 = F_j = \frac{\text{variance explained by } X_j}{\Sigma e^2/(n-k-1)}.$$

The regression as a whole has k degrees of freedom; the variation explained by each variable has one degree of freedom. Thus

$$\text{variation in } Y \text{ explained by } X_j = F_j \cdot \Sigma e^2/(n-k-1)$$

$$= t_j^2 \cdot \text{RSS}/(n-k-1),$$

where RSS = residual sum of squares.

The total sum of squares (TSS), being the sum of the sums of squares explained by each independent variable and the residual sum of squares, is thus

$$\text{TSS} = \frac{\text{RSS}}{(n-k-1)} \cdot (t_1^2 + t_2^2 + \ldots + t_k^2) + \text{RSS}$$

$$= \text{RSS}\{t_1^2/(n-k-1) + t_2^2/(n-k-1) + \ldots + t_k^2/(n-k-1) + 1\}$$

From this *analysis of variance*, it is thus possible to make statements of the form: 'of the total variation in Y, $p\%$ was explained by X_1, $q\%$ by X_2 and $r\%$ was unexplained'. Even more simply, the explained variation divides in the proportions

$$t_1^2/\Sigma t^2 : t_2^2/\Sigma t^2 : \ldots : t_k^2/\Sigma t^2$$

so that the relative contributions of each of the independent variables can be computed directly from the t-statistics. Finally, $F_j (= t_j^2)$ with $(1, n-k-1)$ degrees of freedom can be used to test the significance of the contribution of X_j.

4.7. As well as being used to make inferences about the true values of the parameters being estimated, a regression equation may also be used for prediction. Consider first a simple regression

$$\hat{Y} = \hat{\alpha} + \hat{\beta}X.$$

Suppose that we wish to predict, within a confidence interval, the value of Y which would be associated with a given value of X, say X_0. Then consider the value of Y given by the estimated regression line

$$\hat{Y}_0 = \hat{\alpha} + \hat{\beta}X_0.$$

The true value Y_0 will differ from $\hat{Y}_0$ for two reasons: first, because the regression line $\hat{\alpha} + \hat{\beta}X$ is only an estimate of the true line $\alpha + \beta X$, and, secondly, because Y_0 will differ even from the value given by the true line $\alpha + \beta X_0$ because of the random error u. We thus have to compare

$$\hat{Y}_0 = \hat{\alpha} + \hat{\beta}X_0$$

with the true value

$$Y_0 = \alpha + \beta X_0 + u_0.$$

The difference is

$$Y_0 - \hat{Y}_0 = \alpha - \hat{\alpha} + (\beta - \hat{\beta})X_0 + u_0$$

and thus, since

$$E(Y_0 - \hat{Y}_0) = 0, \quad \text{since } E(\hat{\alpha}) = \alpha, \ E(\hat{\beta}) = \beta,$$

and $E(u_0) = 0$, Y_0 is an unbiased predictor of Y_0.

The variance of the prediction error is

$$E\{(\hat{Y}_0 - Y_0) - E(\hat{Y}_0 - Y_0)\}^2 = E(\hat{Y}_0 - Y_0)^2$$
$$= E(\hat{\alpha} + \hat{\beta}X_0 - \alpha - \beta X_0 - u_0)^2$$
$$= E(u_0^2) + E\{(\hat{\alpha} - \alpha) + (\hat{\beta} - \beta)X_0\}^2$$

(since u_0 is independent of the $u_1 \ldots u_n$ disturbances influencing $\hat{\alpha}, \hat{\beta}$)

$$= \sigma^2 + \text{var}(\hat{\alpha}) + X_0^2 \text{var}(\hat{\beta}) + 2X_0 \text{covar}(\hat{\alpha}, \hat{\beta}) \tag{4.1}$$
$$= \sigma^2(1 + 1/n + \bar{X}^2/\Sigma x^2 + X_0^2/\Sigma x^2 - 2X_0\bar{X}/\Sigma x^2)$$
$$= \sigma^2\{1 + 1/n + (X_0 - \bar{X})^2/\Sigma x^2\}. \tag{4.2}$$

From eqn (4.1) it will be seen that the variance of a forecast can be regarded as consisting of two parts: σ^2, representing the innate randomness of the true values Y, and the remainder, representing the variance of the predictor Y_0 about its mean $E(Y_0)$. If we were interested in predicting the *mean* value of Y_0 for given X_0, that is, the average value which would be obtained from repeated observations with the same value of X_0, the innate disturbance would vanish, and we would obtain a variance

$$\text{var}(\hat{Y}_0) = \sigma^2\left\{\frac{1}{n} + \frac{(X_0 - \bar{X})^2}{\Sigma x^2}\right\}$$

Confidence intervals are obtained by substituting the estimated variance of the error terms,

$$s^2 = \frac{1}{n-2}\Sigma e^2$$

for σ^2, taking the square root to obtain the standard error of the prediction, and using the appropriate value of t to construct the interval.

The expression (4.2) is readily generalized.

In the case of two independent variables, X_{1i} and X_{2i},

$$\text{var}(\hat{Y}_0) = \sigma^2(1 + 1/n) + (X_{10} - \bar{X}_1)^2 \text{ var}(\hat{\beta}_1) + (X_{20} - \bar{X}_2)^2 \text{ var}(\hat{\beta}_2) +$$
$$2(X_{10} - \bar{X}_1)(X_{20} - \bar{X}_2) \text{ covar}(\hat{\beta}_1\hat{\beta}_2).$$

And in the case of m independent variables,

$$\text{var}(\hat{Y}_0) = \sigma^2(1 + 1/n) + \Sigma(X_{k0} - \bar{X}_k) \text{ var}(\hat{\beta}_k) + 2\Sigma(X_{j0} - \bar{X}_j)(X_{k0} - \bar{X}_k)$$
$$\text{covar}(\hat{\beta}_j, \hat{\beta}_k), \quad j, k = 1, 2, \ldots m, \quad j < k.$$

Further reading

J. Kmenta, *Elements of econometrics*, Chapter 5. Macmillan, New York (1971).
C. F. Christ, *Econometric models and methods*, Chapter X. Wiley, New York (1966).
R. L. Anderson and T. A. Bancroft, *Statistical theory in research*, Chapters 11 and 12. McGraw-Hill, New York (1952).

<table>
<tr><td>**5**</td><td># Multicollinearity and principal components</td></tr>
</table>

5.1. Consider the standard regression model with two independent variables:

$$Y = \alpha + \beta_1 X_1 + \beta_2 X_2 + u,$$

where the error term has the familiar desirable properties. The OLS estimator of β_1 is

$$\hat{\beta}_1 = \frac{\Sigma x_1 y \Sigma x_2^2 - \Sigma x_2 y \Sigma x_1 x_2}{\Sigma x_1^2 \Sigma x_2^2 - (\Sigma x_1 x_2)^2} \tag{5.1}$$

and its variance is

$$\text{var}(\hat{\beta}_1) = \frac{\sigma^2 \Sigma x_2^2}{\Sigma x_1^2 \Sigma x_2^2 - (\Sigma x_1 x_2)^2}. \tag{5.2}$$

What effect does the presence of a high degree of correlation between X_1 and X_2 have on the estimates of β_1 and β_2 and their variances? Suppose first that this correlation is perfect, that is, that one variable is simply a linear function of the other. Intuitively, we should expect $\hat{\beta}_1$ and $\hat{\beta}_2$ to be indeterminate, and this is easily shown to be the case. If $X_2 = a + kX_1$ (and thus $x_2 = kx_1$), then

$$\hat{\beta}_1 = \frac{\Sigma x_1 y (k^2 \Sigma x_1^2) - (k\Sigma x_1 y)(k\Sigma x_1^2)}{\Sigma x_1^2 (k^2 \Sigma x_1^2) - k^2 (\Sigma x_1^2)^2} = \frac{0}{0}$$

Correspondingly, the denominator (but not the numerator) of eqn (5.2) becomes zero and the variance of $\hat{\beta}_1$ becomes infinite.

Informally, it will be clear that if the correlation between X_1 and X_2 is high but not perfect, the expression for $\hat{\beta}_1$ will become the ratio of two very small numbers, so that the estimate of β_1 will become highly uncertain, while the denominator of eqn (5.2) will approach zero and so the variance of $\hat{\beta}_1$ will become very large.

Formally, suppose that $x_2 = kx_1 + v$, where v is uncorrelated with x_1, so that the correlation between X_1 and X_2 becomes greater the smaller is the variance of v compared with that of X_1. Then, reverting to the expression derived earlier (§3.2) for $\hat{\beta}_1$ in relation to β_1,

$$\hat{\beta}_1 = \beta_1 + \frac{\Sigma x_1 (u - u) \Sigma x_2^2 - \Sigma x_1 x_2 \Sigma x_2 (u - u)}{\Sigma x_1^2 \Sigma x_2^2 - (\Sigma x_1 x_2)^2}$$

we can substitute for x_2 to obtain

$$\hat{\beta}_1 = \beta_1 + \frac{\Sigma x_1(u-u)\Sigma(kx_1+v)^2 - \Sigma x_1(kx_1+v)\Sigma(kx_1+v)(u-u)}{\Sigma x_1^2\Sigma(kx_1+v)^2 - \{\Sigma x_1(kx_1+v)\}^2}$$

$$= \beta_1 + \frac{\Sigma x_1(u-u)(k\Sigma x_1 v + \Sigma v^2) - \Sigma uv(k\Sigma x_1^2 + \Sigma x_1 v)}{\Sigma x_1^2\Sigma v^2 - (\Sigma x_1 v)^2}$$

Taking expectations,

$$E(\hat{\beta}_1) = \beta_1 + \frac{kE(\Sigma x_1 u \Sigma x_1 v) + E(\Sigma x_1 u \Sigma v^2) - kE(\Sigma uv \Sigma x_1^2) - E(\Sigma uv \Sigma x_1 v)}{\Sigma x_1^2\Sigma v^2 - (\Sigma x_1 v)^2}$$

$= \beta_1$, since, with u and v independently distributed about zero,

$$E(u) = E(v) = E(uv) = 0.$$

Thus the OLS estimate of β_1 is unbiased. The OLS formula for the variance of $\hat{\beta}_1$ is

$$\text{var}(\hat{\beta}_1) = \frac{\sigma^2 \Sigma x_2^2}{\Sigma x_1^2\Sigma x_2^2 - (\Sigma x_1 x_2)^2}$$

But we have already seen that with $x_2 = kx_1 + v$, the denominator reduces to $\Sigma x_1^2\Sigma v^2 - (\Sigma x_1 v)^2$, so that

$$\text{var}(\hat{\beta}_1) = \sigma^2 \frac{k^2\Sigma x_1^2 + 2k\Sigma x_1 v + \Sigma v^2}{\Sigma x_1^2\Sigma v^2 - (\Sigma x_1 v)^2}$$

$$= \sigma^2 \frac{k^2\Sigma x_1^2 + \Sigma v^2}{\Sigma x_1^2\Sigma v^2},$$

since x_1 and v are uncorrelated.

Hence

$$\text{var}(\hat{\beta}) = \sigma^2 \left(\frac{k^2}{\Sigma v^2} + \frac{1}{\Sigma x_1^2} \right)$$

$$= \sigma^2 \left(\frac{k^2}{n\sigma_v^2} + \frac{1}{\Sigma x_1^2} \right).$$

Note that when collinearity is nearly perfect, $\sigma_v^2 \to 0$ and the variance of $\hat{\beta}_1$ becomes very great. At the other limit, there is no collinearity when $k = 0$; in this case, the variance of $\hat{\beta}_1$ becomes $\sigma^2/\Sigma x_1^2$, the variance of the simple regression coefficient of Y on X_1. Provided that σ_v^2 is non-zero (that is, that the collinearity between X_1 and X_2 is not perfect) however, the OLS estimators of β_1 and β_2 will be consistent, since they are unbiased and their variances will tend to zero as the sample size n tends to infinity.

5.2. It is also worth noting that the OLS estimator of σ^2, $s^2 = \Sigma e^2/(n-3)$, remains unbiased despite the presence of a high degree of collinearity. Consider the expectation of Σe^2. Using the expansions developed in §3.3 above,

$$E(\Sigma e^2) = (\sigma^2/D)[2\Sigma x_1^2 \Sigma x_2^2 - 2(\Sigma x_1 x_2)^2 + 2\{\Sigma x_1^2 \Sigma x_2^2 - (\Sigma x_1 x_2)^2\}] + (n-1)\sigma^2$$

(where $D = \Sigma x_1^2 \Sigma x_2^2 - (\Sigma x_1 x_2)^2$)

$$= (n-3)\sigma^2.$$

Thus s^2 remains an unbiased estimator of σ^2.

5.3. Testing for the presence of multicollinearity is not altogether straightforward. It is sometimes suggested that the presence of 'high' standard errors in the estimated coefficients should give adequate warning that there is multicollinearity, but the question is, 'high' compared with what? If we are testing whether a particular coefficient is significantly different from zero, the fact that it appears not to be, given its 'high' standard error, can only be taken as indicating the presence of multicollinearity if we have already prejudged the hypothesis which is being tested by assuming that the coefficient 'ought not' to be insignificant.

In the case where there are only two explanatory variables, of course, the correlation coefficient between the two can be computed and this will directly indicate whether collinearity is high. The expression for the variance of $\hat{\beta}_1$ is

$$\text{var}(\hat{\beta}_1) = \frac{\sigma^2 \Sigma x_2^2}{\Sigma x_1^2 \Sigma x_2^2 - (\Sigma x_1 x_2)^2}$$

which can be written, on dividing top and bottom by Σx_2^2,

$$\text{var}(\hat{\beta}_1) = \frac{\sigma^2}{\Sigma x_1^2 - (\Sigma x_1 x_2)^2/\Sigma x_2^2}$$

$$= \frac{\sigma^2}{\Sigma x_1^2 (1 - r_{12}^2)}$$

where r_{12}^2 is the squared coefficient of correlation between X_1 and X_2.

Thus the fact that var$(\hat{\beta}_1)$ is calculated to be 'high' is only evidence of collinearity if the reason is that r_{12}^2 is close to unity.

When there are more than two explanatory variables, the problem of testing for the presence of multicollinearity becomes much more difficult. This is because it is quite possible for three (or more) variables to be highly collinear even though the simple correlations between each pair are low. As an extreme example, consider a set of three explanatory variables which can only take the values 0 or 1 as follows:

Period	X_1	X_2	X_3
1	1	0	0
2	0	1	0
3	0	0	1
4	1	0	0
.	.	.	.
.	.	.	.
.	.	.	.

Then for large n, $\overline{X}_1 = \overline{X}_2 = \overline{X}_3 = 1/3$,

and $$\Sigma x_1^2 = \Sigma x_2^2 = \Sigma x_3^2 = 2n/9,$$

while $$\Sigma x_1 x_2 = \Sigma x_2 x_3 = \Sigma x_1 x_3 = -n/9,$$

so that $$r_{12} = r_{23} = r_{13} = -0 \cdot 5.$$

Yet since $X_1 = 1 - X_2 - X_3$, collinearity between the set as a whole is perfect.

Thus for more than two explanatory variables, the simple correlation coefficients may be quite misleading as indicators of the degree of multicollinearity which is present. An obvious extension of the method can, however, be used when there are more than two explanatory variables. In this case, multicollinearity simply means that at least one of the explanatory variables is very close to being a linear function of one or more of the other explanatory variables. Thus if we regress each of the Xs on the remaining Xs, the occurrence of a high R^2 will indicate the presence of multicollinearity.

Tests of this kind suffer from an inevitable degree of vagueness which is inherent in the nature of the problem. Each of the R^2s will normally be non-zero. What is to count as a particularly 'high' value? When multicollinearity is a serious problem, the estimates of some of the βs will be highly uncertain, but we cannot predict from this the values of the $\hat{\beta}$s which would be obtained if multicollinearity were absent.

5.4. The obvious solution to the problem of multicollinearity is to attempt to find additional data which reduce the collinearity. Since economists generally have little choice about the data available, this may seem unhelpful. Nevertheless, choices are occasionally possible: the use of cross-section data to supplement multicollinear time-series data is a good example. In demand studies in which demand for a good is held to depend on income and relative price, collinearity between income and relative price time-series may be avoided in cross-section analysis, in which relative price is, by definition, fixed and demand may be related directly to income. From the cross-section analysis, it may thus be possible to estimate

$$q_i = \hat{\alpha}_1 + \hat{\beta}_1 Y_i + e_i$$

and then to use the estimate of $\hat{\beta}_1$ in the time-series analysis by 'correcting' quantity demanded for the effect of income:

$$(q_t - \hat{\beta}_1 Y_t) = \hat{\alpha}_2 + \hat{\beta}_2 p_t$$

(where i denotes cross-section and t times-series data, q is quantity demanded, Y is income and p is relative price).

Note, though, that such a solution may be unacceptable on economic grounds if it is inappropriate to apply a coefficient estimated on the basis of cross-section behaviour to the analysis of time-series behaviour. The relative income hypothesis, for example, suggests that there may be just such a problem: the estimation of $\hat{\beta}_1$ from cross-section data may reflect not the effect of changes in absolute income, but only of variations in income relative to the mean. If the mean is itself shifting over time, $\hat{\beta}_1$ will be an inappropriate estimate of the effect on demand of changes in income over time.

A more general use of the availability of both cross-section and time-series data is to pool both sets of data. In this case, as well as the economic problems there may be difficult econometric problems, notably if the assumptions made about the error terms are different in the two cases.

5.5. A different solution, which does not depend on the acquisition of fresh data, is to use the method of principal components. For any plausible number of variables, the algebra becomes impossible to handle without matrix notation, but the principle can be illustrated quite simply for the case of two variables.

Suppose, in general, that we have a set of explanatory variables which are highly multicollinear. The method of principal components is a technique of forming a small number of linear combinations of the variables, each of which is uncorrelated with the rest but which together account for the greater part of the variance of the original variables. Symbolically, we form new variables, z_{jt}, where

$$z_{1t} = a_1 x_{1t} + a_2 x_{2t} + \ldots + a_k x_{kt}$$
$$z_{2t} = b_1 x_{1t} + b_2 x_{2t} + \ldots + b_k x_{kt}$$

$$\cdot \qquad \cdot \qquad \cdot \qquad \cdot$$
$$\cdot \qquad \cdot \qquad \cdot \qquad \cdot$$
$$\cdot \qquad \cdot \qquad \cdot \qquad \cdot$$

so that the k original explanatory variables x_k are replaced by a limited number of zs, each of which is a different linear combination of the original xs. The problem is to choose the as so that z_1 accounts for as much as possible of the variance of the xs, then to choose the bs so that the second component z_2 accounts for as much as possible of the remaining variance, subject to the condition that z_2 be uncorrelated with z_1, and so on. A further constraint must be that $a_1^2 + a_2^2 + \ldots a_k^2 = 1$, for otherwise the variance of z_1 could be increased indefinitely simply by increasing each of the a's by the same factor. We thus have to maximize Σz_{1t}^2 subject to $\Sigma a^2 = 1$. To do this, we form the Lagrangean

$$\mathcal{L} = \Sigma z_1^2 - \lambda(\Sigma a^2 - 1)$$

(dropping the observation subscript t).

To illustrate, assume that we have just two variables, x_1 and x_2. Then

$$\mathcal{L} = \Sigma(a_1 x_1 + a_2 x_2)^2 - \lambda(\Sigma a^2 - 1)$$
$$= a_1^2 \Sigma x_1^2 + a_2^2 \Sigma x_2^2 + 2a_1 a_2 \Sigma x_1 x_2 - \lambda(\Sigma a^2 - 1).$$

Differentiating with respect to a_1 and a_2:

$$\frac{\partial \mathcal{L}}{\partial a_1} = 2a_1 \Sigma x_1^2 + 2a_2 \Sigma x_1 x_2 - 2\lambda a_1$$

$$\frac{\partial \mathcal{L}}{\partial a_2} = 2a_2 \Sigma x_2^2 + 2a_1 \Sigma x_1 x_2 - 2\lambda a_2.$$

Setting these equal to zero and rearranging:

$$\left.\begin{aligned}
a_1 \Sigma x_1^2 + a_2 \Sigma x_1 x_2 = \lambda a_1 \\
a_2 \Sigma x_2^2 + a_1 \Sigma x_1 x_2 = \lambda a_2
\end{aligned}\right\} \tag{5.3}$$

or

$$\left.\begin{aligned}
a_1 (\Sigma x_1^2 - \lambda) + a_2 \Sigma x_1 x_2 = 0 \\
a_1 \Sigma x_1 x_2 + a_2 (\Sigma x_2^2 - \lambda) = 0
\end{aligned}\right\} \tag{5.4}$$

from which

$$\lambda^2 - (\Sigma x_1^2 + \Sigma x_2^2)\lambda + \Sigma x_1^2 \Sigma x_2^2 - (\Sigma x_1 x_2)^2 = 0.$$

This is a quadratic in λ which, when solved in terms of the known sums of squares and cross-products of the xs, will give two roots. In order to maximize the variance of z_1, we choose the larger of the roots; eqns (5.4) together with the constraint $a_1^2 + a_2^2 = 1$ allow us to solve for a_1 and a_2 and thus to form the first principal component $z_{1t} = a_1 x_{1t} + a_2 x_{2t}$.

To take a numerical example, suppose that $\Sigma x_1^2 = 1 \cdot 5$, $\Sigma x_2^2 = 4 \cdot 5$ and $\Sigma x_1 x_2 = 2$. Then $r_{12} = 2/\sqrt{\{(1 \cdot 5)(4 \cdot 5)\}} = 0 \cdot 77$,

and $$\lambda^2 - (4 \cdot 5 + 1 \cdot 5)\lambda + (6 \cdot 75 - 4) = 0,$$

that is, $$\lambda^2 - 6\lambda + 2 \cdot 75 = 0$$

giving $(\lambda - 5 \cdot 5)(\lambda - 0 \cdot 5) = 0$; $\lambda = 5 \cdot 5$ or $0 \cdot 5$. Taking the larger root and substituting in eqns (5.4):

$$-4a_1 + 2a_2 = 0,$$

$$2a_1 - a_2 = 0,$$

that is, $$a_2 = 2a_1.$$

We also have the constraint $a_1^2 + a_2^2 = 1$,

that is, $$a_1^2 + 4a_1^2 = 1, \quad \text{whence} \quad a_1 = \frac{1}{\sqrt{5}} \quad \text{and} \quad a_2 = \frac{2}{\sqrt{5}}$$

Thus the first principal component is

$$z_{1t} = \frac{1}{\sqrt{5}} x_{1t} + \frac{2}{\sqrt{5}} x_{2t}.$$

Note that the variation of the original xs was $\Sigma x_1^2 + \Sigma x_2^2 = 6$ while the variation of the first principal component is

$$\Sigma z_1^2 = \frac{1}{5}\Sigma x_1^2 + \frac{4}{5}\Sigma x_2^2 + \frac{4}{5}\Sigma x_1 x_2$$

$$= 5 \cdot 5,$$

so that the first principal component accounts for 92 % of the variance of the original variables. (Note that in fact it follows directly from eqns (5.3) that λ is equal to Σz_1^2.)

The second principal component can be derived in the same way. There is now an additional constraint, namely, that $\Sigma ab = 0$, since z_2 is to be uncorrelated with z_1. Thus the Lagrangean is

$$\mathscr{L} = \Sigma(b_1 x_1 + b_2 x_2)^2 - \lambda_2(\Sigma b^2 - 1) - \mu \Sigma ab,$$

and it can easily be shown that, on differentiating with respect to the bs, $\mu = 0$ and λ_2 is the other root of the original quadratic in λ found earlier.

In general, with k explanatory variables, there can be derived a kth order equation in λ. The λs are known as the latent roots or eigenvalues of the data; computer programs are generally available for their extraction and for the formation of the associated principal components (also known as latent vectors or eigenvectors).

If the original set of xs was highly collinear, the first few principal components are likely to account for most of the total variance of the xs. In this way, a large number of variables can be reduced to a handful for use in a regression analysis without the loss of any significant explanatory power, and with the precision of the estimates of the regression coefficients relatively great since the principal components are totally uncorrelated with each other. Note, though, that the xs must all be expressed in the same units if the notion of each component's 'explaining' a part of their total variance is to mean anything.

5.6. Is the method of principal components really helpful in dealing with the problem of multicollinearity? There are two ways of answering this. First, if the principal components used (which on the face of it are, from an economic point of view, arbitrary combinations of the original variables) can be given an economic meaning, then the regression on the components may as it stands mean something. For example, in an early economic application of the method, Stone found that 97·5 % of the variance of 17 different series taken from the U.S. national income accounts was accounted for by the first three principal components. (The reference is given under *Further reading* below.) But 'it is important to remember that the individual principal factors are mere arithmetical abstractions chosen for certain convenient algebraic properties. There is no general reason for identifying them singly with underlying causes' (Stone, *loc. cit.*, p. 19). Nevertheless, Stone found that the first component was highly correlated with the level of national income, the second with the rate of change of income, and the third with time. In such a case, the economist might thus use the method in order simply to pick out those few 'genuine' variables which need to be incorporated in his analysis. The problem remains, however, if the first few components are not readily identifiable with economic magnitudes.

A more general use relies on the fact that, given the coefficients from the regression on the first few components, these can be transformed back to coefficients on the original variables. Thus if a regression of Y is performed on the first component of a set of x's:

$$\hat{Y} = \hat{\alpha} + \hat{\beta} z_1,$$

where

$$z_1 = a_1 x_1 + a_2 x_2 + \ldots + a_k x_k,$$

then we can write

$$\hat{Y} = \hat{\alpha} + \hat{\beta} a_1 x_1 + \hat{\beta} a_2 x_2 + \ldots + \hat{\beta} a_k x_k.$$

If the regression had been performed directly on the xs the estimates of the parameters would have been unbiased but, given multicollinearity, highly imprecise (that is, have had large sample variances). The use of the principal components method will give estimates of $(\hat{\beta} a_1)$ etc., which, although biased (since some of the components have been suppressed), will apparently have much smaller variances, since the as are constants and the estimate of β will be quite precise. Clearly it is quite possible that the bias will be small enough for the method to be preferable to direct regression analysis, in that it may produce smaller mean squared errors on the coefficients. Unfortunately, this argument rests on a mistaken premise. It is not correct to treat the as as given constants. They are in effect coefficients which could easily be quite different yet still explain almost as much of the variance of the xs, if the latter are indeed highly collinear. The apparent precision of the coefficients of the transformed equation thus vanishes when the imprecision of the coefficients of the principal components is taken into account.

5.7. Multicollinearity thus remains a largely intractable problem. Unless new data can be found and utilized plausibly, or unless the principal components approach suggests an obvious limitation of the explanatory variables, the imprecise estimates of parameters obtained when collinearity is severe cannot be avoided.

Further reading

On multicollinearity, see:
J. Johnston, *Econometric methods* (2nd. edn), Chapter 5.7. McGraw-Hill, New York (1972).

On principal components and other multivariate methods, see:
P. J. Dhrymes, *Econometrics*, Chapter 2. Harper and Row, New York (1970).

<table>
<tr><td>

6

</td><td>

Miscellaneous single-equation problems

</td></tr>
</table>

6.1. So far, we have not departed from the standard regression model

$$Y_i = \alpha + \beta_1 X_{1i} + \beta_2 X_{2i} + \ldots + u_i,$$

where the Xs are given and may be treated as fixed values (that is, they do not contain a random error term and are not correlated with u_i), and where the disturbance u_i has zero expected value, constant variance, and is genuinely random, that is,

$$E(u_i) = 0; \quad E(u_i u_j) = \sigma^2, \quad i = j$$
$$= 0, \quad i \neq j.$$

In this chapter and the next we consider the problems which arise if not all these conditions are satisfied.

6.2. First we consider what happens if the Xs contain an error term – the problem of *errors in variables*. The model given above is still assumed to be the true model, but in performing the regression analysis the data on the explanatory variables consist not of the true values of X_i but of the observed values X_i' where

$$X_i' = X_i + v_i,$$

that is, each observed value of X is the sum of the true but unknown value X_i and an error term v_i which might be thought of as, for example, an error in measuring X_i. Thus instead of being able to estimate the true relationship

$$Y_i = \alpha + \beta X_i + u_i$$

in the case of one explanatory variable, we are forced to replace X_i by X_i'. What effect will this have on the OLS estimators? The OLS estimator for β will be

$$\hat{\beta} = \frac{\Sigma x_i' y_i}{\Sigma x_i'^2}$$

where $x_i' = X_i' - \overline{X}_i'$ and thus $x_i' = x_i + (v_i - \bar{v})$.

Thus
$$\hat{\beta} = \frac{\Sigma \{x_i + (v_i - \bar{v})\} y_i}{\Sigma \{x_i + (v_i - \bar{v})\}^2}$$

$$= \frac{\Sigma x_i y_i + \Sigma(v_i - \bar{v}) y_i}{\Sigma x_i^2 + 2\Sigma x_i(v_i - \bar{v}) + \Sigma(v_i - \bar{v})^2}.$$

Now since $\Sigma x_i = \Sigma y_i = 0$, and since v_i is assumed to be uncorrelated both with the true values X_i and with Y_i, in the limit as the sample size tends to infinity,

$$\hat{\beta} \text{ tends to } \frac{\Sigma x_i y_i}{\Sigma x_i^2 + \Sigma v_i^2}$$

that is, $\hat{\beta}$ tends to $\dfrac{\beta}{1 + (\Sigma v_i^2 / \Sigma x_i^2)} = \dfrac{\beta}{1 + (\sigma_v^2 / \sigma_x^2)}$

where σ_v^2 is the variance of v_i and σ_x^2 is the variance of X. Thus $\hat{\beta}$ is biased even for an infinitely large sample: $\hat{\beta}$ is an inconsistent estimator of β.

6.3. A good example of the problem is provided by the permanent income hypothesis. Here, the level of consumption, C, is determined by the level of permanent income, Y^p. Measured income is the sum of permanent and transitory income, and the transitory component of income is a random element with zero mean and is uncorrelated with C and Y^p. Then the true consumption function is

$$C = \alpha + \beta Y^p + u.$$

(Note that it makes no difference whether u is regarded as an equation disturbance or as an 'error' in C which might be thought of as transitory consumption.) If this is estimated using OLS and measured income, the estimate of the marginal propensity to consume will, in the limit, be as before

$$\hat{\beta} = \frac{\beta}{1 + (\sigma_t^2 / \sigma_p^2)}$$

where, with $Y = Y^p + Y^t$, σ_t^2 is the variance of transitory income and σ_p^2 the variance of permanent income. If the variance of Y^t is, say, one-tenth that of Y^p, $\hat{\beta}$ will underestimate β by about 10%. OLS estimation of the consumption function will thus tend to underestimate the true marginal propensity to consume.

6.4. In practice, of course, it is unlikely that one will be able to estimate the ratio of the variance of the measurement error to that of the true value of X. One may, however, be able to guess at the ratio of the variance of the measurement error so that of the disturbance u, especially if the latter arises solely from measurement error in Y. For instance, if both X and Y are time-series taken from the national accounts, it may be possible to gauge the relative accuracy of the two series. In this case, we have the model

$$Y = \alpha + \beta X + u,$$

where we have data on $X' = X + v$ and we know the ratio of σ_u^2 to σ_v^2, say λ.

The model we estimate is thus based on the exact relation

$$y = \beta x$$

in which the data are $y' = y + u$ and $x' = x + v$. Thus the true relation can be written in terms of observed values of x and y:

$$y' - u = \beta(x' - v)$$

or
$$y' = \beta x' + (u - \beta v).$$

If we multiply through first by x', then by y', and sum:

$$\Sigma x'y' = \beta \Sigma x'^2 + \Sigma(u - \beta v)x' \tag{6.1}$$

$$\Sigma y'^2 = \beta \Sigma x'y' + \Sigma(u - \beta v)y'. \tag{6.2}$$

Now
$$\Sigma(u - \beta v)x' = \Sigma xu - \beta \Sigma xv + \Sigma uv - \beta \Sigma v^2,$$

which in the limit is equal to $-\beta \Sigma v^2$, since all other terms vanish, and similarly:

$$\Sigma(u - \beta v)y' = \Sigma(u - \beta v)(y + u)$$

$$= \Sigma yu - \beta \Sigma yv + \Sigma u^2 - \beta \Sigma vu$$

$$= \Sigma u^2.$$

Thus

$$\Sigma x'y' = \beta \Sigma x'^2 - \beta \Sigma v^2 \tag{6.1a}$$

$$\Sigma y'^2 = \beta \Sigma x'y' + \Sigma u^2 \tag{6.2a}$$

giving two equations in the three unknowns β, Σu^2, Σv^2. If we know that $\sigma_u^2/\sigma_v^2 = \lambda$, then eqn (6.2a) becomes

$$\Sigma y'^2 = \beta \Sigma x'y' + \lambda \Sigma v^2 \tag{6.2b}$$

and on substitution for Σv^2 from eqn (6.2b) into eqn (6.1a),

$$\Sigma x'y' = \beta \Sigma x'^2 - \frac{\beta}{\lambda} \Sigma y'^2 + \frac{\beta^2}{\lambda} \Sigma x'y'$$

or
$$\beta^2 - \beta \left(\frac{\Sigma y'^2}{\Sigma x'y'} - \lambda \frac{\Sigma x'^2}{\Sigma x'y'} \right) - \lambda = 0.$$

This quadratic will have two roots, one of which will be positive and the other negative (this follows from the fact that λ must be positive). Which root to choose depends on the covariance between X and Y; if this is positive then β will be positive too, and vice-versa.

It is worth noting that as λ tends to infinity, or $1/\lambda$ tends to zero, so that the error in X vanishes, eqn (6.1a) gives the normal OLS estimator of β, while as λ tends to zero, so that the error in X is the only error, eqn (6.2a) gives the unbiased estimator of β as that obtained by regressing X on Y. $\lambda = 1$ represents, of course, the case where the variances of the errors in X and Y are equal: this case is known as orthogonal regression.

6.5. A second way of coping with the problem of inconsistency when X is subject to error is the method of *instrumental variables*. Suppose we can find a variable Z which is correlated with the true value of X but uncorrelated with the error in the equation and with the error in X. Given that

$$y = \beta x + u',$$

where x is the true value and $u' = u - \bar{u}$, then

$$y = \beta(x' - v') + u'$$
$$= \beta x' + u' - \beta v',$$

where x' is the observed value of x and $v' = v - \bar{v}$. On multiplying through by z and summing.

$$\Sigma yz = \beta \Sigma x'z + \Sigma z(u' - \beta v').$$

Now in the limit, as $n \to \infty$, $\Sigma zu' = \Sigma zv' = 0$, and thus

$$\hat{\beta} = \frac{\Sigma yz}{\Sigma x'z}$$

is a consistent estimator of β. Note that OLS can be considered as a special case of instrumental variables when X is used as an instrument for itself. X in this case satisfies the conditions required for an instrumental variable since it is (perfectly) correlated with itself and is assumed to be independent of the error term u.

6.6. Another assumption of the standard regression model which may not always be satisfied is $E(u_i^2) = \sigma^2$, constant for all i. It is often plausible to suppose that the variance of the error term increases as the scale of the variables increases. For example, if u_i represents an error of measurement in Y_i, the degree of error might be expected to rise *pari passu* with Y, so that $E(u_i^2) \propto Y_i^2$. In general, when $E(u_i^2)$ is not constant, the disturbances are said to be *heteroscedastic*.

What happens if OLS is applied in such a case? First, OLS estimates will still be unbiased, for

$$\hat{\beta} = \frac{\Sigma x_i y_i}{\Sigma x_i^2} = \frac{\Sigma x_i(Y_i - \bar{Y})}{\Sigma x_i^2}$$
$$= \frac{\Sigma x_i Y_i}{\Sigma x_i^2},$$

since $\Sigma x_i = 0$ and thus $\bar{Y}\Sigma x_i = 0$. Thus

$$\hat{\beta} = \frac{\Sigma x_i(\alpha + \beta X_i + u_i)}{\Sigma x_i^2}$$

$$= \frac{\alpha \Sigma x_i + \beta \Sigma x_i X_i + \Sigma x_i u_i}{\Sigma x_i^2}$$

and $E(\hat{\beta}) = \beta$, since $\Sigma x_i = 0$ and $E(\Sigma x_i u_i) = \Sigma x_i E(u_i) = 0$, since it is still assumed that $E(u_i) = 0$.

For the variance of $\hat{\beta}$,

$$\text{var}(\hat{\beta}) = E(\hat{\beta} - \beta)^2 \quad (\text{since } E(\hat{\beta}) = \beta)$$

$$= E\left[\left(\frac{\Sigma x_i u_i}{\Sigma x_i^2}\right)^2\right]$$

$$= \frac{1}{(\Sigma x_i^2)^2} \cdot E(\Sigma x_i^2 u_i^2)$$

(since $E(u_i u_j) = 0$, $i \neq j$)

$$= \frac{1}{(\Sigma x_i^2)^2} \cdot \Sigma x_i^2 E(u_i^2)$$

and without an assumption about the value of $E(u_i^2)$ we can go no further.

Suppose that $E(u_i^2)$ varies with X_i^2, so that

$$E(u_i^2) = kX_i^2,$$

or, for convenience,

$$E(u_i^2) = \sigma^2 X_i^2,$$

where σ^2 is a constant.

Then
$$\text{var}(\hat{\beta}) = \frac{1}{(\Sigma x_i^2)^2} \cdot \Sigma[x_i^2 \sigma^2 X_i^2]$$

$$= \sigma^2 \frac{\Sigma x_i^2 X_i^2}{(\Sigma x_i^2)^2}$$

and if σ^2 were known, the variance could be computed. Even if σ^2 is unknown, however, it is possible to show that OLS produces relatively inefficient estimates. The original model was

$$Y_i = \alpha + \beta X_i + u_i,$$

where $E(u_i^2) = \sigma^2 X_i^2$.

Note that if we divide through by X_i, we obtain

$$\frac{Y_i}{X_i} = \alpha \frac{1}{X_i} + \beta + \frac{u_i}{X_i}$$

and the transformed error term is homoscedastic, since its variance is

$$E\left(\frac{u_i}{X_i}\right)^2 = \frac{1}{X_i^2}\,E(u_i^2) = \sigma^2$$

Thus OLS applied to the transformed equation will produce best linear unbiased estimates. To compare the variances of the two methods, we may take a simple numerical example. Suppose that X takes the value $(1, 2, 3)$. Then direct application of OLS to the original model gives

$$\mathrm{var}\,(\hat{\beta}) = \frac{10}{4}\sigma^2 = 2{\cdot}5\sigma^2.$$

Application of OLS to the transformed equation

$$Y_i' = \beta + \alpha X_i' + u_i'$$

(where $Y' = Y/X$, $X' = 1/X$, $u' = u/X$) gives

$$\mathrm{var}\,(\hat{\beta}) = \sigma^2 \left(\frac{1}{n} + \frac{\overline{X}'^2}{\Sigma x'^2}\right)$$

(since β is the constant term)

$$= \sigma^2 \left(\frac{1}{3} + \frac{121}{78}\right)$$

$$= 1{\cdot}9\sigma^2$$

The variance of $\hat{\beta}$ obtained by transforming the equation is thus substantially lower than if OLS were applied to the original equation.

However, it does not follow that if OLS is applied to a model in which the disturbances are heteroscedastic, the conventional formula for the variance of $\hat{\beta}$ will always overstate the 'true' variance of $\hat{\beta}$. This is because σ^2 is unknown, and must be estimated from the residuals of the fitted equation. It can be shown that there is no general answer to the question of whether the variance of $\hat{\beta}$ computed from the conventional formula

$$\mathrm{var}\,(\hat{\beta}) = \frac{1}{n-2}\frac{\Sigma e^2}{\Sigma x^2}$$

will be greater or less than the true value when OLS is applied to a model with a heteroscedastic disturbance. Whether the variance of $\hat{\beta}$ so calculated is greater or less than the true variance depends on whether the covariance between the u_i^2 and the x_i^2 is negative or positive. There is generally no reason to presuppose either case. For instance, if $E(u_i^2)$ increases with X_i or X_i^2, then although $E(u_i^2)$ will increase as we pass from low to high values of X, x^2 (the squared deviation from the mean) will first decrease and then increase. Thus whether the covariance between u_i^2 and x_i^2 is positive or negative cannot in general be predicted. (See the paper by Bacon listed under *Further reading* below.)

6.7. Another common, and rather intractable, problem in econometrics is that of specification error. In practice, any economic variable is likely to be influenced by a host of factors not all of which will be included in the regression analysis. There are various reasons why some variables should be excluded. First, the inclusion of a large number of explanatory variables will of course reduce the number of degrees of freedom in the analysis, thus making the estimates of the parameters imprecise. Secondly, some explanatory factors may not be quantifiable, and thus are difficult to incorporate into a numerical analysis. Thirdly, of course, variables may be omitted 'by mistake': their relevance is unrecognized.

Informally, it is obvious that the effect of leaving out an important explanatory variable will be to bias the estimates of the effects of the variables which are included, since the latter will be 'doing the work' in part of the excluded factors. The extent of the bias will depend both on the size of the influence which is ignored (in effect, on the 'true' coefficient of the variable) and on the extent to which the included variables are correlated with the excluded ones and are thus able to act as proxies. We observed earlier that one rationalization of the error term in a regression equation was to say that it reflected the influence of omitted explanatory factors; this rationalization is only justified if such influences taken together can reasonably be expected to have a quasi-random effect on the dependent variable. This will not be the case if one (or more) of the omitted variables both is significantly correlated with the dependent variable and has an effect which is not 'cancelled out' by another omitted variable, leaving a quasi-random net influence.

To take the simplest example, suppose that the true model is

$$Y = \alpha + \beta_1 X_1 + \beta_2 X_2 + u$$

but the variable X_2 is omitted in the regression analysis, so that the fitted line is

$$\hat{Y} = \hat{\alpha}' + \hat{\beta}_1' X_1$$

The OLS estimator, $\hat{\beta}_1'$, is

$$\hat{\beta}_1' = \frac{\Sigma y x_1}{\Sigma x_1^2}$$

$$= \frac{\Sigma x_1 (\beta_1 x_1 + \beta_2 x_2 + u - \bar{u})}{\Sigma x_1^2}$$

$$= \beta_1 + \beta_2 \frac{\Sigma x_1 x_2}{\Sigma x_1^2} + \frac{\Sigma x_1 (u - \bar{u})}{\Sigma x_1^2}$$

And

$$E(\hat{\beta}_1') = \beta_1 + \beta_2 \frac{\Sigma x_1 x_2}{\Sigma x_1^2} \tag{6.3}$$

since

$$E\{\Sigma x_1 (u - \bar{u})\} = \Sigma x_1 E(u) - \bar{u}\Sigma x_1$$
$$= 0.$$

From eqn (6.3) it will be seen that $\hat{\beta}'_1$ is a biased estimate of β_1, the true coefficient of X_1, and, as one would expect, the bias depends both on the sign and size of the true but omitted influence of X_2 on Y (represented by β_2), and on the extent of the correlation between X_1 and X_2. Thus if X_1 and X_2 are positively correlated and β_2 is positive, β_1 will be overestimated; it will in part be doing the work which the term $\beta_2 X_2$ should have been doing.

If X_1 and X_2 are not correlated, the estimate of β_1 obtained from the simple regression of Y on X_1 will be unbiased, but the failure to include X_2 in the regression equation is still important, for it means that the estimate of the variance of β_1 obtained from the simple regression will be overstated. This incorrect estimated variance will be

$$s^2(\hat{\beta}'_1) = \frac{s^2}{\Sigma x_1^2}$$

where

$$s^2 = \Sigma e^2/(n-2)$$
$$= \{1/(n-2)\}\Sigma(y - \hat{\beta}'_1 x_1)^2$$
$$= \{1/(n-2)\}\Sigma\{(\beta_1 - \hat{\beta}'_1)x_1 + \beta_2 x_2 + u - \bar{u}\}^2.$$

Thus

$$E(s^2) = \{1/(n-2)\}\{\mathrm{var}(\hat{\beta}'_1)\Sigma x_1^2 + \beta_2^2\Sigma x_2^2 + (n-1)\sigma^2 + 2\beta_2(\beta_1 - E\hat{\beta}'_1)\Sigma x_1 x_2\}$$

$$= \{1/(n-2)\}\left\{\mathrm{var}(\hat{\beta}'_1)\Sigma x_1^2 + \beta_2^2\Sigma x_2^2 + (n-1)\sigma^2 - 2\beta_2^2 \frac{(\Sigma x_1 x_2)^2}{\Sigma x_1^2}\right\}$$

(using eqn 6.3)

$$= \{1/(n-2)\}\{\mathrm{var}(\hat{\beta}'_1)\Sigma x_1^2 + \beta_2^2\Sigma x_2^2 + (n-1)\sigma^2 - 2\,\mathrm{var}(\hat{\beta}'_1)\Sigma x_1^2\}$$

$$= \{1/(n-2)\}\{-\mathrm{var}(\hat{\beta}'_1)\Sigma x_1^2 + \beta_2^2\Sigma x_2^2 + (n-1)\,\mathrm{var}(\hat{\beta}'_1)\Sigma x_1^2\}$$

(if X_1 and X_2 are uncorrelated)

$$= \mathrm{var}(\hat{\beta}'_1)\Sigma x_1^2 + \frac{\beta_2^2 \Sigma x_2^2}{n-2}$$

Then

$$s^2(\hat{\beta}'_1) = \mathrm{var}(\hat{\beta}'_1) + \beta_2^2 \frac{\Sigma x_2^2}{(n-2)\Sigma x_1^2},$$

that is, for finite samples, the computed variance of the estimate of β_1 based on a simple regression will overstate the true variance. The hypothesis $\beta_1 \neq 0$ will thus tend to be rejected more often than it should.

6.8. Another case of mis-specification occurs when a true relationship which is non-linear is estimated by means of a linear regression. In general, if the true relationship is

$$Y = f(X) + u \tag{6.4}$$

then under certain conditions it can be approximated by

$$Y = \alpha + \beta_1 X + \beta_2 X^2 + \beta_3 X^3 + \ldots + u$$

(using Taylor's expansion, the conditions being that $f(X)$ is continuous and possesses continuous derivatives).

If this is estimated by

$$Y = \hat{\alpha} + \hat{\beta} X$$

then the problem becomes one of omitted variables, where the omitted variables are $X^2, X^3 \ldots$ etc., and the analysis developed in §6.7 above applies.

If the form of eqn (6.4) is known as *a priori*, it may be possible to find a transformation which will directly reduce it to a linear model. For example, suppose a demand study is being conducted and it is assumed that quantity demanded depends on price with a constant price elasticity of demand. Then

$$q = f(p) \tag{6.5}$$

with the elasticity

$$\frac{dq}{dp} \cdot \frac{p}{q} = \beta. \tag{6.6}$$

Eqn (6.5) can be written

$$\frac{dq}{q} = \beta \cdot \frac{dp}{p}$$

and, on integration,

$$\ln q = \alpha + \beta \ln p. \tag{6.7}$$

Thus β can be estimated directly by regressing $\ln q$ on $\ln p$. The functional form in this case is

$$q = e^{\alpha} \cdot p^{\beta}. \tag{6.8}$$

Note, though, that only if the error in eqn (6.8) is multiplicative with mean unity will the error term in eqn (6.7) be additive with zero mean.

It is not always possible to find a suitable transformation, though logarithmic, semi-logarithmic and reciprocal transformations have often proved useful in economic contexts. For example,

$$Y = \alpha + \beta X^{\gamma}$$

cannot be linearized in such a way as to enable α, β, and γ to be estimated by OLS.

Further reading

On errors in variables, see:

J. Johnston, *Econometric methods* (2nd edn), Chapter 9. McGraw-Hill, New York (1972).

E. Malinvaud, *Statistical methods of econometrics* (2nd edn), Chapter 10. North-Holland, Amsterdam (1970).

On heteroscedasticity, see:

J. Johnston, *op. cit.*, Chapter 7.3.

R. W. Bacon, A note on the effect of heteroscedasticity, *Bull. Oxford Univ. Inst. Econ. Stat.* (May 1971).

On specification error, see:

J. Kmenta, *Elements of econometrics*, Chapter 10.4. Macmillan, New York (1971).

7.1. A further assumption of the standard regression model is that $E(u_i u_j) = 0$, $i \neq j$. This assumption can of course be false in many different ways. Here we consider one particularly important case, common in time-series studies, namely that the error in one period is related to the error in the previous period, so that

$$u_t = \rho u_{t-1} + v_t.$$

In other words, each period's error is a fraction ρ of the previous period's error together with a genuinely independent random element, v_t. This is known as first-order autocorrelation (or serial correlation) of the errors; it is of course possible to specify much more complicated schemes of second or higher order, such as

$$u_t = \rho_1 u_{t-1} + \rho_2 u_{t-2} + v_t, \text{ etc.}$$

How will autocorrelation affect OLS estimates? First, we note that the v_t have the usual properties of a random disturbance, that is,

$$E(v_t) = 0, \quad E(v_t v_{t-\tau}) = \sigma^2, \quad \tau = 0$$
$$= 0, \quad \tau \neq 0.$$

Now
$$u_t = \rho u_{t-1} + v_t$$
$$= \rho^2 u_{t-2} + \rho v_{t-1} + v_t, \text{ etc.},$$

that is,
$$u_t = v_t + \rho v_{t-1} + \rho^2 v_{t-2} + \ldots$$

and thus
$$E(u_t) = E(v_t) + \rho E(v_{t-1}) + \rho^2 E(v_{t-2}) + \ldots$$
$$= 0$$

since
$$E(v_t) = 0 \text{ for all } t.$$

Furthermore,
$$E(u_t^2) = E(v_t^2) + \rho^2 E(v_{t-1}^2) + \rho^4 E(v_{t-2}^2) + \ldots$$

(since $E(v_t v_{t-\tau}) = 0, \tau \neq 0$)

and so
$$\sigma_u^2 = E(u_t^2) = \sigma^2(1 + \rho^2 + \rho^4 + \ldots)$$
$$= \sigma^2/(1 - \rho^2)$$

Next,
$$E(u_t u_{t-1}) = E\{(v_t + \rho v_{t-1} + \ldots)(v_{t-1} + \rho v_{t-2} + \ldots)\}$$
$$= \rho E(v_{t-1}^2) + \rho^3 E(v_{t-2}^2) + \ldots$$

(since again $E(v_t v_{t-\tau}) = 0$, $\tau \neq 0$).

Thus $\qquad\qquad E(u_t u_{t-1}) = \rho\sigma^2/(1 - \rho^2) = \rho\sigma_u^2.$

And in general, $\qquad\quad E(u_t u_{t-\tau}) = \rho^\tau \sigma_u^2.$

Now in the simple regression

$$Y = \alpha + \beta X + u$$

when first-order autocorrelation is present, the OLS estimate of β is unbiased, since

$$\hat\beta = \frac{\Sigma x_t y_t}{\Sigma x_t^2}$$

$$= \frac{\Sigma x_t(\beta x_t + u_t - \bar u)}{\Sigma x_t^2}$$

and $\qquad\qquad\qquad E(\hat\beta) = \beta$

since $\Sigma x_t = 0$ and $E(u_t) = 0$ for all t.

The variance of $\hat\beta$ is igven by

$$\mathrm{var}(\hat\beta) = E\{\hat\beta - E(\hat\beta)\}^2$$

$$= E\left\{\frac{\Sigma x_t(u_t - u)}{\Sigma x_t^2}\right\}^2$$

$$= \frac{1}{(\Sigma x_t^2)^2} E\{\Sigma x_t^2 u_t^2 + 2\Sigma x_t x_{t-1} u_t u_{t-1} + 2\Sigma x_t x_{t-2} u_t u_{t-2} + \ldots\}$$

$$= \frac{1}{(\Sigma x_t^2)^2}\{\sigma_u^2\Sigma x_t^2 + 2\rho\sigma_u^2\Sigma x_t x_{t-1} + 2\rho^2\sigma_u^2\Sigma x_t x_{t-2} + \ldots\}$$

$$= \frac{\sigma_u^2}{\Sigma x_t^2} + \frac{\sigma_u^2}{\Sigma x_t^2}\left\{2\rho\frac{\Sigma x_t x_{t-1}}{\Sigma x_t^2} + 2\rho^2\frac{\Sigma x_t x_{t-2}}{\Sigma x_t^2} + \ldots\right\}.$$

This expression shows that the OLS estimator of $\mathrm{var}(\hat\beta)$ consists of the estimator which would be correct if the errors were not serially correlated — $\sigma_u^2/\Sigma x_t^2$ — together with the sum of a series of terms involving both ρ and terms of the form $\Sigma x_t x_{t-\tau}/\Sigma x_t^2$. Thus, given σ_u^2, the variance of $\hat\beta$ will depend on the value of this sum. If ρ lies between 0 and 1 (positive serial correlation) and if the x's are positively correlated, the conventional formula $\sigma_u^2/\Sigma x_t^2$ will underestimate the true variance of $\hat\beta$. The xs will tend to be positively correlated, of course, in most time-series in which x is subject to a growth trend. For example, suppose that x_t follows a first-order autoregressive scheme with parameter λ, then

$$\mathrm{var}(\hat\beta) = \frac{\sigma_u^2}{\Sigma x_t^2} + \frac{\sigma_u^2}{\Sigma x_t^2}\{2\rho\lambda + 2\rho^2\lambda^2 + \ldots\}$$

$$= \frac{\sigma_u^2}{\Sigma x_t^2} \left\{ 1 + 2\rho\lambda(1 + \rho\lambda + \rho^2\lambda^2 + \ldots) \right\}$$

$$= \frac{\sigma_u^2}{\Sigma x_t^2} \left\{ \frac{1 + \rho\lambda}{1 - \rho\lambda} \right\}.$$

Thus for ρ and λ both between 0 and 1, the variance of $\hat{\beta}$ will be greater than that given by the conventional formula, while for either $\rho = 0$ (no serial correlation of errors) or $\lambda = 0$ (no serial correlation in the explanatory variable), the conventional formula is unbiased.

There is one further problem: σ_u^2 is not known, but must be estimated from the regression residuals. When the errors are autocorrelated, these residuals are on balance likely to underestimate the true errors if the xs are positively correlated. This may be seen graphically (Fig. 7.1).

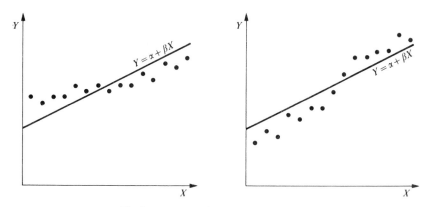

Fig. 7.1. Autocorrelated disturbance term

In both cases, the errors are positively correlated, and the OLS line will fit spuriously well. For a more formal proof, note that

$$\Sigma e_t^2 = \Sigma(y_t - \hat{\beta}x_t)^2$$

$$= \Sigma\left\{ -(\hat{\beta} - \beta)x_t + u_t - \bar{u} \right\}^2$$

$$= \text{var}(\hat{\beta})\Sigma x_t^2 + \Sigma(u_t - \bar{u})^2 - 2(\hat{\beta} - \beta)\Sigma x_t(u_t - \bar{u}).$$

Thus since $\quad E\left\{ \Sigma(u_t - \bar{u})^2 \right\} = (n - 1)\sigma_u^2$

and $\quad E\left\{ (\hat{\beta} - \beta)\Sigma x_t(u_t - \bar{u}) \right\} = (1/\Sigma x_t^2)E\left\{ \Sigma x_t(u_t - \bar{u}) \right\}^2 = \Sigma x_t^2 \cdot \text{var}(\hat{\beta}),$

$$E(\Sigma e_t^2) = (n - 1)\sigma_u^2 - \sigma_u^2 \left\{ 2\rho\frac{\Sigma x_t x_{t-1}}{\Sigma x_t^2} + 2\rho\frac{\Sigma x_t x_{t-2}}{\Sigma x_t^2} + \ldots \right\}.$$

Again, if both u_t and x_t are positively serially correlated, the OLS estimator of σ_u^2 will tend to underestimate the true value of σ_u^2.

Thus on both counts, and for the same reasons, the conventional formula for the variance of $\hat{\beta}$ will give a spuriously precise value if u_t and x_t are subject to positive serial correlation.

7.2. Methods of estimating regression equations more satisfactorily when the errors are serially correlated are bound to depend on estimating the unknown parameter ρ. If ρ were known, the equation could be transformed so as to give a new relationship in which the errors were not autocorrelated, for, given that

$$Y_t = \alpha + \beta x_t + u_t$$

and

$$u_t = \rho u_{t-1} + v_t,$$

where v_t is serially independent, then by lagging the equation one period and subtracting from the original equation, we obtain

$$Y_t - \rho Y_{t-1} = \alpha(1 - \rho) + \beta(x_t - \rho x_{t-1}) + u_t - \rho u_{t-1}$$

$$= \alpha' + \beta(x_t - \rho x_{t-1}) + v_t,$$

The solution would thus be to form the new variables

$$Y'_t = Y_t - \rho Y_{t-1} \quad \text{and} \quad X'_t = X_t - \rho X_{t-1}$$

and perform the regression on these transformed variables.

However, ρ is generally unknown. An obvious way of estimating ρ is to use the residuals from the equation estimated by OLS. For simplicity, assume no constant term in the equation.

Then

$$y_t = \hat{\beta} x_t + e_t,$$

compared with the true equation

$$y_t = \beta x_t + u_t,$$

where

$$u_t = \rho u_{t-1} + v_t$$

and v_t has zero expected value, constant variance and is not serially correlated. The suggested method of estimating ρ is to use the e_t as estimates of the u_t, giving

$$\hat{\rho} = \frac{\Sigma e_t e_{t-1}}{\Sigma e_{t-1}^2}$$

$$= \frac{\Sigma(y_t - \hat{\beta} x_t)(y_{t-1} - \hat{\beta} x_{t-1})}{\Sigma(y_{t-1} - \hat{\beta} x_{t-1})^2}$$

$$= \frac{\Sigma\{(\beta - \hat{\beta}) x_t + u_t\}\{(\beta - \hat{\beta}) x_{t-1} + u_{t-1}\}}{\Sigma\{(\beta - \hat{\beta}) x_{t-1} + u_{t-1}\}^2}$$

$$= \frac{(\beta - \hat{\beta})^2 \Sigma x_t x_{t-1} + (\beta - \hat{\beta})(\Sigma x_t u_{t-1} + \Sigma u_t x_{t-1}) + \Sigma u_t u_{t-1}}{(\beta - \hat{\beta})^2 \Sigma x_{t-1}^2 + 2(\beta - \hat{\beta})\Sigma x_{t-1} u_{t-1} + \Sigma u_{t-1}^2}$$

Now $\hat{\beta}$, the OLS estimator of β, is unbiased as we have seen, that is, $E(\hat{\beta} - \beta) = 0$. Thus

$$E(\hat{\rho}) = \frac{\text{var}\,\hat{\beta}\Sigma x_t x_{t-1} + E(\Sigma u_t u_{t-1})}{\text{var}\,\hat{\beta}\Sigma x_{t-1}^2 + E(\Sigma u_{t-1}^2)}$$

$$= \frac{\{\sigma^2(\hat{\beta})/\sigma_u^2\}\Sigma x_t x_{t-1} + \rho}{\{\sigma^2(\hat{\beta})/\sigma_u^2\}|\Sigma x_{t-1}^2 + 1}$$

Thus $\hat{\rho}$ is a biased estimator of ρ. If the xs are not serially correlated, so that $\Sigma x_t x_{t-1} \to 0$, $\hat{\rho}$ will underestimate ρ even in the limit, since the first term in the denominator remains positive. It is, however, possible to use this technique as the first stage of an iterative process: compute $\hat{\rho}$ as just described, regress $(y_t - \hat{\rho}y_{t-1})$ on $(x_t - \hat{\rho}x_{t-1})$, use the residuals from this second regression to form a new estimate of the remaining serial correlation, form new variables . . . and so on, stopping the process when it has converged, that is, when the residuals cease to be serially correlated. The conventional OLS formulae will then give consistent estimates of the error variances.

7.3. Testing for serial correlation is usually done by means of the Durbin–Watson statistic. Again, this involves the residuals from the OLS estimation of the equation. The statistic is defined as

$$d = \frac{\Sigma(e_t - e_{t-1})^2}{\Sigma e_t^2}$$

Informally, on expanding the numerator we obtain

$$d = \frac{\Sigma e_t^2 + \Sigma e_{t-1}^2 - 2\Sigma e_t e_{t-1}}{\Sigma e_t^2}$$

so that in the absence of serial correlation, when the expected value of $\Sigma e_t e_{t-1}$ is equal to zero, $d = 2$. For positive serial correlation, $0 \leqslant d < 2$ and for negative serial correlation $2 < d \leqslant 4$. The actual sampling distribution of d is, however, complex and Durbin and Watson were unable to provide unique boundaries to decide whether d in a particular case is or is not significantly different from 2. There remain two bands, above and below 2, where the hypothesis of serial correlation can be neither confirmed nor rejected at any given level of significance.

7.4. Another common problem in time-series analysis arises when the influence of X on Y is not complete in one period but is spread over several periods – the problem of *distributed lags*.

The general form of such a model would then be

$$Y_t = \alpha + \beta_0 X_t + \beta_1 X_{t-1} + \ldots + \beta_n X_{t-n} + u_t \tag{7.1}$$

where the influence of X on Y is pread over n periods. If the number of periods is not too great, such a model might be estimated as it stands, since there may be enough degrees of freedom left to allow all the parameters to be estimated satisfactorily. Even so, multicollinearity among the lagged X's may be severe. A common solution to this problem is to postulate a certain shape for the pattern of the 'weights' β_i over time and then to transform the equation in such a way as considerably to reduce the number of parameters to be estimated. We consider here two particular ways of specifying the lag distribution which have been frequently used: the geometrically distributed lag and the polynomial (Almon) lag.

7.5. If the influence of X is likely to be greatest in the current period and to decline at a uniform proportional rate as we go back in time, eqn (7.1) can be written

$$Y_t = \alpha + \beta(X_t + \lambda X_{t-1} + \lambda^2 X_{t-2} + \ldots) + u_t \tag{7.2}$$

with $0 \leqslant \lambda < 1$. The average lag is then

$$\frac{0 + 1\lambda + 2\lambda^2 + 3\lambda^3 + \ldots}{1 + \lambda + \lambda^2 + \lambda^3 + \ldots} = \frac{\lambda}{1 - \lambda},$$

since, calling the numerator N and the denominator D,

$$N - \lambda N = \lambda + \lambda^2 + \lambda^3 + \ldots = \lambda/(1 - \lambda),$$

and thus $N = \lambda/(1 - \lambda)^2$, and $D = 1/(1 - \lambda)$.

Neglecting the error term for the moment, if eqn (7.2) is lagged one period and multiplied by λ, we obtain

$$\lambda Y_{t-1} = \alpha\lambda + \beta(\lambda X_{t-1} + \lambda^2 X_{t-2} + \ldots),$$

and when this is subtracted from eqn (7.2):

$$Y_t - \lambda Y_{t-1} = \alpha(1 - \lambda) + \beta X_t$$

or $$Y_t = \alpha(1 - \lambda) + \beta X_t + \lambda Y_{t-1}. \tag{7.3}$$

Thus only three parameters — the constant, β, and λ — need to be estimated; the problems of lack of degrees of freedom and of multicollinearity are enormously reduced. Unfortunately, other problems now intrude. Their nature depends in part on the specification of the error term, which has so far been suppressed and which is governed by the underlying economic reasoning which justifies the imposition of a geometrically-distributed lag.

Reverting to eqn (7.2), it might be possible to assume that this represents quite straightforwardly the economic position. Consumption, for example, may depend partly on current income and partly on past periods' incomes with a gradually declining influence, and on a disturbance term. But it follows that when the equation is transformed for estimation to the form (7.3), the new disturbance term will have the form $u_t - \lambda u_{t-1}$ and the problem of autocorrelation intrudes.

A second simple case would result if the transformed equation (7.3) were itself taken as directly reflecting the economic mechanism: consumption could be thought to depend partly on current income and partly, because of habit or inertia, on the previous period's level of consumption, together with a stochastic disturbance. Thus the error term in eqn (7.3) would be free from serial dependence.

Two further important cases arise when less naive assumptions are made about the justification of the geometric form of the distributed lag. These are the assumptions of a stock-adjustment model and of an adaptive expectations model. The stock-adjustment model supposes that the equilibrium level of consumption depends directly on current income, but actual consumption adjusts, in any period, by only a fraction of the gap between equilibrium consumption and the previous period's actual level of consumption. Thus

$$C_t^* = \alpha + \beta Y_t$$

where C_t^* is the equilibrium level of consumption in period t, and

$$C_t - C_{t-1} = \lambda(C_t^* - C_{t-1}) + u_t;$$

the actual change in consumption is only a fraction λ of the gap between equilibrium consumption and previous actual consumption, together with an error term u_t. Then on substitution,

$$C_t = \alpha\lambda + \beta\lambda Y_t + (1 - \lambda)C_{t-1} + u_t$$

which is of the geometrically distributed lag form, but in which there is no presumption on this account that u_t will be autocorrelated.

Alternatively, suppose that consumption in the current period depends on expected (or, in another possible interpretation, 'permanent') income:

$$C_t = \alpha + \beta Y_t^* + u_t,$$

where Y_t^* is expected income, and that expectations are revised in each period by a fraction λ of the gap between actual income and previously expected income:

$$Y_t^* - Y_{t-1}^* = \lambda(Y_t - Y_{t-1}^*).$$

Then, on substitution,

$$C_t = \alpha\lambda + \beta\lambda Y_t + (1 - \lambda)C_{t-1} + u_t - (1 - \lambda)u_{t-1},$$

and in this case, although the form of the relationship between the variables is the same, it now contains a disturbance which is not serially independent. Note that both these models employ a device common in econometric work: that of forming a hypothesis about the way in which unobservable quantities (such as C_t^* or Y_t^*) are dependent on (and reducible to functions of) observed variables.

We can thus distinguish two general cases in estimating equations containing a lagged dependent variable of the form

$$Y_t = \alpha + \beta X_t + \gamma Y_{t-1} + u_t:$$

(a)
$$E(u_t) = 0, \; E(u_t u_{t-\tau}) = \sigma_u^2, \; \tau = 0$$
$$= 0, \quad \tau \neq 0$$

(b)
$$u_t = v_t - \lambda v_{t-1},$$

where v_t is genuinely random with zero expected value and variance σ_v^2, and thus

$$E(u_t) = 0, \quad E(u_t u_{t-\tau}) = \sigma_v^2(1 + \lambda^2), \; \tau = 0$$
$$= -\lambda \sigma_v^2 \qquad \tau = 1$$
$$= 0, \qquad\quad \tau \geqslant 2.$$

(a) In this case, although the u_t are not serially correlated, problems do arise because of the inclusion of the variable Y_{t-1}, which is not independent of $u_{t-1}, u_{t-2}, \ldots$. It can be shown (though the proof is not easy) that the OLS estimators of the parameters will have a bias, usually small, which vanishes as the sample size becomes infinite. Generally speaking, the estimate of β will be biased downwards and that of γ upwards.

(b) In this case, when the error term is not serially independent, it has been shown that the parameter estimates are not only biased, but the bias does not vanish as the sample size tends to infinity.

7.6. The second general method of imposing a definite pattern on the 'shape' of the distributed lag is to make the successive weights lie on a polynomial of specified degree. This method is particularly useful when, in contrast to the geometrically distributed lag, the influence of a variable may be expected first to rise and then to fall in an inverted V shape. This may well be appropriate, for example, in the case of the response of investment to a change in output.

In order to employ the method, it is necessary to specify *a priori* both the degree of the polynomial and the number of periods before the weights return to zero. The strength of the method in reducing the number of variables in the regression equation lies in the fact that a polynomial of degree n has $(n + 1)$ parameters and is thus fully defined by fitting to $(n + 1)$ points. Thus a quadratic is defined by three points, and so on. Computer programs are often available for the estimation of polynomial lags; in order to illustrate the method, we take the very simple case where the polynomial is of degree 2 (quadratic), and the weights return to zero in the third period. We thus have

$$Y_t = \alpha + \beta(w_0 X_t + w_1 X_{t-1} + w_2 X_{t-2}) + u_t$$

in which, since the w_i lie on a quadratic:

$$w_i = \lambda_0 + \lambda_1 i + \lambda_2 i^2, \quad i = -1, 0, 1 \dots 3,$$

but subject to $w_{-1} = w_3 = 0$.

Hence

$$w_{-1} = \lambda_0 - \lambda_1 + \lambda_2 = 0,$$

$$w_3 = \lambda_0 + 3\lambda_1 + 9\lambda_2 = 0,$$

from which

$$4\lambda_0 + 12\lambda_2 = 0,$$

$$\lambda_0 = -3\lambda_2,$$

and

$$\lambda_1 = \lambda_0 + \lambda_2$$

$$= -2\lambda_2.$$

Now

$$w_0 X_t = \lambda_0 X_t,$$

$$w_1 X_{t-1} = (\lambda_0 + \lambda_1 + \lambda_2) X_{t-1},$$

and

$$w_2 X_{t-2} = (\lambda_0 + 2\lambda_1 + 4\lambda_2) X_{t-2}.$$

Thus

$$Y_t = \alpha + \beta\{-3\lambda_2 X_t + (-3\lambda_2 - 2\lambda_2 + \lambda_2)X_{t-1} + (-3\lambda_2 - 4\lambda_2 + 4\lambda_2)X_{t-2}\} + u_t$$

$$= \alpha + \beta\lambda_2(-3X_t - 4X_{t-1} - 3X_{t-2}) + u_t.$$

We thus regress Y_t on a composite variable made up in the way shown; the quadratic is fitted to three points, two determined by constraining $w_{-1} = w_3 = 0$ and the third being fitted implicitly by the regression analysis. Note that β and λ_2 are not separately identified; we are likely to be interested in the total effect of a unit change in X on Y after all lags have worked out, and this is given by

$$\hat\beta \Sigma \hat w_i = \hat\beta\{3\lambda_0 + (1 + 2)\lambda_1 + (1^2 + 2^2)\lambda_2\}$$

$$= -10(\hat\beta\lambda_2)$$

so that the separation of $\hat\beta$ from $\hat\lambda_2$ is unnecessary.

Further reading

J. Johnston, *Econometric methods* (2nd edn), Chapters 8 (autocorrelation) and 10 (distributed lags). McGraw-Hill, New York (1972).

E. Malinvaud, *Statistical methods of econometrics* (2nd edn), Chapters 13 (autocorrelation) and 14 – 15 (distributed lags). North-Holland, Amsterdam (1970).

Z. Griliches, Distributed lags – a survey, *Econometrica* (January 1967).

8.1. Although we have concentrated on single equations so far, it is clear that in economics most relationships are parts of a wider system in which the dependence between two variables is rarely one-way. Whether it is in any particular case a reasonable simplification to ignore the simultaneity of the system and to use single-equation methods is always difficult to decide, but there are of course many cases in which simultaneity cannot be ignored. Simultaneity raises two kinds of problem, the first concerned with *identification* and the second with *estimation*.

8.2. In order to consider the identification problem, consider a competitive market in which both supply and demand are functions of price:

$$Q_d = \alpha + \beta P + u$$

$$Q_s = \gamma + \delta P + v$$

(where u and v are independently distributed disturbances with the usual desirable properties). We also have the market clearing condition

$$Qd = Qs.$$

From this set of relationships, we can derive (by eliminating first Q and then P) two *reduced form* equations for price and quantity:

$$P = \frac{\gamma - \alpha}{\beta - \delta} + \frac{v - u}{\beta - \delta}$$

$$Q = \frac{\beta\gamma - \alpha\delta}{\beta - \delta} + \frac{\beta v - \delta u}{\beta - \delta}$$

These are particularly simple reduced forms since they contain no variables; thus

$$E(P) = \bar{P} = \frac{\gamma - \alpha}{\beta - \delta}$$

$$E(Q) = \bar{Q} = \frac{\beta\gamma - \alpha\delta}{\beta - \delta}$$

so that the parameters of the two reduced form equations (the constant terms) can be estimated simply as P and Q. But it is clearly impossible to estimate from these two reduced form equations the four structural parameters α, β, γ and δ. The system is said to be under-identified. Only if two of the four parameters could be specified *a priori* would the system be identified.

8.3. Now suppose that demand, as well as depending on price, depends on income:

$$Q_d = \alpha + \beta P + \lambda Y + u$$

$$Q_s = \gamma + \delta P.$$

The reduced form equations are now

$$P = \frac{\alpha - \gamma}{\delta - \beta} + \frac{\lambda}{\delta - \beta} \, Y + \frac{u - v}{\delta - \beta}$$

$$Q = \frac{\delta \alpha - \beta \gamma}{\delta - \beta} + \frac{\lambda \delta \, Y}{\delta - \beta} + \frac{\delta u - \beta v}{\delta - \beta}$$

or

$$P = a + bY + u'$$

$$Q = c + dY + v'.$$

Now considering the supply equation

$$Q_s = \gamma + \delta P,$$

it can be seen from the two reduced form equations that

$$\delta = d/b$$

and δ is thus determinate, and also that

$$c = \frac{\delta \alpha - \beta \gamma}{\delta - \beta}$$

$$= \delta \, \frac{\alpha - \gamma}{\delta - \beta} + \frac{\delta \gamma - \beta \gamma}{\delta - \beta}$$

$$= \delta a + \gamma,$$

and thus γ is also determined, since a, c, and δ are known. The supply equation is thus identified. The demand equation remains under-identified, however: it is still impossible to obtain unique values for α, β, and λ.

Note that in this case the inclusion of an exogenous variable (income) in the *demand* equation enabled the *supply* equation to become identified. The reason for this is best seen diagrammatically (Fig. 8.1).

In Fig. 8.1(a), where demand does not depend on income, the data scatter will be concentrated at the intersection of the two lines; it will be impossible to fit two independent lines through the scatter and identify them as supply and demand equations. In Fig. 8.1(b) variations in income cause the demand schedule to shift, and the resulting scatter will trace out the *supply* schedule, which thus becomes identified. Note that if supply also depended on income, both equations would be under-identified again, for we should be back to the original problem but in three dimensions rather than two.

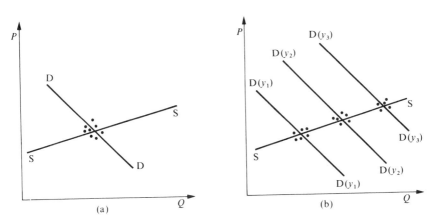

Fig. 8.1. The identification problem

8.4. Now suppose that demand depends not only on price and income but also on some other price (of a complement or substitute). Then

$$Q_d = \alpha + \beta P + \lambda Y + \pi P' + u$$

$$Q_s = \gamma + \delta P + v,$$

where P' is the new price variable. Then we obtain reduced forms

$$P = \frac{\alpha - \gamma}{\delta - \beta} + \frac{\lambda}{\delta - \beta} Y + \frac{\pi}{\delta - \beta} P' \frac{u - v}{\delta - \beta}$$

$$Q = \frac{\delta\alpha - \beta\gamma}{\delta - \beta} + \frac{\lambda\delta}{\delta - \beta} Y + \frac{\pi\delta}{\delta - \beta} P' + \frac{\delta u - \beta v}{\delta - \beta}$$

or

$$P = a + bY + cP' + u',$$

$$Q = d + eY + fP' + v'.$$

Now it is clearly possible to obtain two separate estimates of δ, one as e/b and another as f/c, from the estimates of the reduced form equations. There is no reason to suppose that the two estimates will coincide, nor is there any reason to prefer one estimate to the other. In this case, the supply equation is said to be *over-identified*. (The demand equation is easily shown to remain under-identified.)

8.5. Testing for identification in a system by means of the manipulation of the reduced form coefficients in order to see whether unique expressions for the structural coefficients can be derived is clearly a tedious business; it would be useful to devise a simpler test. Such a test can be derived and, to do so, we first consider the expressions for the OLS estimators of the reduced form equations. If we revert to the case in which demand depended on price and income, we recall that the supply equation was exactly identified and that the reduced form equations were

$$P = a + bY + u'$$

$$Q = c + dY + v'$$

with δ (the structural coefficient of price in the supply equation) equal to d/b. Now if OLS is applied to the reduced form equations,

$$\hat{d} = \frac{\Sigma qy}{\Sigma y^2} \quad \text{and} \quad \hat{b} = \frac{\Sigma py}{\Sigma y^2}$$

so that

$$\hat{d}/\hat{b} = \frac{\Sigma qy}{\Sigma py}.$$

If this is compared with the original supply equation

$$Q = \gamma + \delta P$$

we note that OLS applied directly would give

$$\hat{\delta} = \frac{\Sigma pq}{\Sigma p^2}$$

so that the estimate of $\hat{\delta}$ obtained from the reduced form equations is exactly what would be obtained by direct estimation of the supply equation but using Y as an instrumental variable for P (see above, §6.5). However, if we attempt to use Y as an instrument in the demand equation we obtain

$$\Sigma qy = \hat{\beta}\Sigma py + \hat{\lambda}\Sigma y^2,$$

and $\hat{\beta}$ and $\hat{\lambda}$ are still indeterminate. Thus Y is only useful as an instrumental variable in the equation in which it does *not* appear as an explanatory variable. This can be generalized to a useful rule (though the proof does require matrix algebra). Suppose we have a system of simultaneous equations in which there are G structural relationships and in which K pre-determined (exogenous or lagged endogenous) variables appear. The typical relationship will then be

$$Y_i = \alpha + \beta_1 Y_1 + \beta_2 Y_2 + \ldots + \beta_{i-1} Y_{i-1} + \beta_{i+1} Y_{i+1} + \ldots +$$
$$+ \beta_G Y_G + \gamma_1 X_1 + \gamma_2 X_2 + \ldots + \gamma_K X_K + u_i$$

where the Ys are endogenous and the Xs predetermined variables. Now some of the βs and γs must be zero, otherwise the whole model would be indeterminate.

The question is, how many of which kind of parameters must be zero for the equation to be exactly identified? The answer is that the number of γs which are zero must be equal to the number of endogenous variables included as explanatory variables in the equation. This counting rule can be expressed in different ways. For instance, an alternative way of putting it is to say that in the right hand side of the equation, the number of excluded predetermined variables must equal the number of included endogenous variables. Or, equivalently, the total number of variables (both endogenous and predetermined) excluded from the right-hand side must equal the number of structural equations in the system.

To illustrate, consider the supply–demand system discussed earlier. In the first case (omitting disturbances)

$$Q_d = \alpha + \beta P$$
$$Q_s = \gamma + \delta P$$

leading to two reduced form equations

$$Q = a$$
$$P = b.$$

The system has two endogenous variables (P and Q) and no predetermined variables. Both supply and demand equations are under-identified: the number of excluded predetermined variables (zero) is less than the number of endogenous variables included on the right-hand side (one).

Now consider the system

$$Q_d = \alpha + \beta P + \gamma Y,$$
$$Q_s = \gamma + \delta P$$

leading to the reduced form equations

$$Q = a + bY,$$
$$P = c + dY.$$

Now the demand equation has zero excluded predetermined variables but includes one endogenous variable in the right-hand side (P) and so is under-identified. The supply equation also includes one endogenous variable on the right-hand side (P), but excludes one predetermined variable (Y) and so is exactly identified. If demand depended on another price, P', as well as on income and own-price, then the demand equation would remain under-identified but the supply equation would be over-identified, since the number of excluded predetermined variables (two) would then be greater than the number of endogenous variables on the right-hand side (one).

8.6. The 'counting rule' is, however, a necessary but not a sufficient condition for identification. Consider the following three-equation system:

(a) $\qquad Y_1 = \alpha_1 + \beta_{12} Y_2 + \gamma_{11} X_1 + \gamma_{12} X_2 + u_1,$

(b) $\qquad Y_2 = \alpha_2 + \beta_{21} Y_1 + \gamma_{21} X_1 + \gamma_{22} X_2 + u_2,$

(c) $\qquad Y_3 = \alpha_3 + \beta_{31} Y_1 + \beta_{32} Y_2 + \gamma_{33} X_3 + u_3.$

The counting rule (or *order condition*) suggests that each equation is exactly identified, for in each case the number of predetermined variables X excluded from the right-hand side is equal to the number of endogenous variables Y included. But in fact the third equation is not part of a simultaneous system at all, for Y_3 does not appear in either of the first two equations. Hence these first two equations form by themselves a simultaneous set in two endogenous and two predetermined variables, and both are under-identified since they each include one endogenous variable on the right-hand size but exclude neither of the predetermined variables.

A further problem in checking identification is of a practical kind. Even with an exactly identified equation, it may turn out on estimation that one of the excluded predetermined variables has estimated coefficients which are not significantly different from zero in any equation of the system. In that case, the variable will be discarded from the system, and the number of excluded predetermined variables in the original equation is reduced by one. That equation then becomes under-identified.

8.7. Problems in estimating systems of simultaneous equations arise in general because the error terms will be correlated with one or more of the explanatory variables in the structural equations. To illustrate this, consider the simple macroeconomic model

$$C = \alpha + \beta Y + u,$$

$$Y = C + I.$$

The model consists of a consumption function and the national income identity in which investment is taken to be exogenous. The error term in the consumption function is assumed to have the familiar desirable properties. From the consumption function, C is correlated with u, and from the income identity, Y is correlated with C. Hence Y is influenced by u and the independent variable and the error term in the consumption function are thus not independent. This means that OLS estimates of the consumption function will be biased, since

$$\hat{\beta} = \frac{\Sigma cy}{\Sigma y^2}$$

$$= \frac{\Sigma(\beta y + u - \bar{u})y}{\Sigma y^2}$$

and thus $E(\hat{\beta}) = \beta + E(\Sigma yu / \Sigma y^2).$

But
$$Y = C + I$$
$$= \alpha + \beta Y + I + u$$
$$= \frac{\alpha}{1 - \beta} + \frac{I}{1 - \beta} + \frac{u}{1 - \beta}$$

and thus
$$E(yu) = \frac{E(u^2)}{1 - \beta} \neq 0.$$

Thus the OLS estimator of β will be biased even in large samples: this is known as *simultaneous equation bias*.

An obvious way of avoiding the problem suggests itself once it is noticed that the structural equation (the consumption function) is exactly identified. It follows that estimates of α and β can be uniquely obtained from estimates of the reduced form.

Solving the two structural equations gives

$$C = \alpha + \beta(C + I) + u$$
$$= \frac{\alpha}{1 - \beta} + \frac{\beta}{1 - \beta} I + \frac{u}{1 - \beta}$$

and
$$Y = \frac{\alpha}{1 - \beta} + \frac{1}{1 - \beta} I + \frac{u}{1 - \beta}$$

Since I and u are completely uncorrelated, estimation of OLS of these reduced forms will give unbiased estimates from which asymptotically unbiased estimates of the structural parameters α and β can be obtained. This method is known as indirect least squares (ILS), and will clearly be useful only in the case of exactly identified equations.

It is worth noting that, as in the case of the exactly identified supply equation discussed in §8.3 above, ILS is equivalent to using the exogenous variable I as an instrumental variable in estimating the consumption function. From the reduced form equation for consumption, we have

$$\frac{\hat{\beta}}{1 - \hat{\beta}} = \frac{\Sigma ci}{\Sigma i^2}$$

that is,
$$\hat{\beta} = \frac{\Sigma ci}{\Sigma ci + \Sigma i^2}$$

and since $y = c + i$, $\Sigma ci + \Sigma i^2 = \Sigma yi$, so that $\hat{\beta} = \Sigma ci / \Sigma yi$, which is the instrumental variable estimator of the consumption function using I as an instrument. Investment satisfies the requirements for an instrumental variable: it is correlated with Y (through the multiplier) but is independent of u (since I is exogenous).

8.8. A second method of coping with the problem of simultaneous equation bias is known as two-stage least squares (2SLS). The first stage is to regress the variable which is correlated with the error term (Y) on the exogenous variable (I). The *calculated* values of Y from this regression will thus no longer depend on the error term but will be simply a linear function of I. These calculated values of Y can then be used in the structural equation in place of the actual values, thereby avoiding the problem of correlation between Y and u. The first regression is thus

$$Y = \hat{\gamma} + \hat{\delta}I + e,$$

where

$$\hat{\delta} = \frac{\Sigma yi}{\Sigma i^2}.$$

The computed values of Y are

$$\hat{Y} = \hat{\gamma} + \hat{\delta}I$$

and these are used in the second stage: the estimation of the consumption function. The OLS estimator of β is then

$$\hat{\beta} = \frac{\Sigma c\hat{y}}{\Sigma \hat{y}^2},$$

and this will be a consistent estimator of β.

In fact, again since the consumption function is exactly identified, the 2SLS estimator is identical with the ILS estimator, for

$$\hat{\delta} = \frac{\Sigma yi}{\Sigma i^2}, \quad \text{and} \quad \hat{y} = \hat{\delta}i,$$

and thus

$$\hat{\beta} = \frac{\Sigma c\hat{y}}{\Sigma \hat{y}^2}$$

$$= \frac{\hat{\delta}\Sigma ci}{\hat{\delta}^2 \Sigma i^2}$$

$$= \frac{\Sigma i^2}{\Sigma yi} \cdot \frac{\Sigma ci}{\Sigma i^2}$$

$$= \frac{\Sigma ci}{\Sigma yi}$$

which is the ILS (and the instrumental variables) estimator.

8.9. In the case of an over-identified equation, we already know that unique values of the structural parameters cannot be obtained from estimates of the parameters of the reduced form equations – indeed this is precisely what over-identification means. The method of indirect least squares is thus no help. The method of two stage least squares, however, can still be employed. In each equation, the endogenous variables on the right-hand side of each structural equation are replaced by their calculated values derived from regression on all the predetermined variables in the system. Since these calculated values are, in the limit, uncorrelated with the equation disturbance, the estimates of the structural parameters will be asymptotically unbiased, unlike the OLS estimators.

Further reading

On the identification problem, see:
A. S. Goldberger, *Econometric theory*, Chapter VII. Wiley, New York (1964).
F. M. Fisher, *The identification problem in econometrics*. McGraw-Hill, New York (1966).

On estimation problems, see:
J. Johnston, *Econometric methods* (2nd edn), Chapter 13. McGraw-Hill, New York (1972).
E. Malinvaud, *Statistical methods of econometrics*, Chapters 19 and 20. North-Holland, Amsterdam (1970).

TABLE 1

THE STANDARD NORMAL DISTRIBUTION

Probabilities for specified values of Z.

z	.00	.01	.02	.03	.04	.05	.06	.07	.08	.09
0.0	.0000	.0040	.0080	.0120	.0160	.0199	.0239	.0279	.0319	.0359
0.1	.0398	.0438	.0478	.0517	.0557	.0596	.0636	.0675	.0714	.0753
0.2	.0793	.0832	.0871	.0910	.0948	.0987	.1026	.1064	.1103	.1141
0.3	.1179	.1217	.1255	.1293	.1331	.1368	.1406	.1443	.1480	.1517
0.4	.1554	.1591	.1628	.1664	.1700	.1736	.1772	.1808	.1844	.1879
0.5	.1915	.1950	.1985	.2019	.2054	.2088	.2123	.2157	.2190	.2224
0.6	.2257	.2291	.2324	.2357	.2389	.2422	.2454	.2486	.2517	.2549
0.7	.2580	.2611	.2642	.2673	.2704	.2734	.2764	.2794	.2823	.2852
0.8	.2881	.2910	.2939	.2967	.2995	.3023	.3051	.3078	.3106	.3133
0.9	.3159	.3186	.3212	.3238	.3264	.3289	.3315	.3340	.3365	.3389
1.0	.3413	.3438	.3461	.3485	.3508	.3531	.3554	.3577	.3599	.3621
1.1	.3643	.3665	.3686	.3708	.3729	.3749	.3770	.3790	.3810	.3830
1.2	.3849	.3869	.3888	.3907	.3925	.3944	.3962	.3980	.3997	.4015
1.3	.4032	.4049	.4066	.4082	.4099	.4115	.4131	.4147	.4162	.4177
1.4	.4192	.4207	.4222	.4236	.4251	.4265	.4279	.4292	.4306	.4319
1.5	.4332	.4345	.4357	.4370	.4382	.4394	.4406	.4418	.4429	.4441
1.6	.4452	.4463	.4474	.4484	.4495	.4505	.4515	.4525	.4535	.4545
1.7	.4554	.4564	.4573	.4582	.4591	.4599	.4608	.4616	.4625	.4633
1.8	.4641	.4649	.4656	.4664	.4671	.4678	.4686	.4693	.4699	.4706
1.9	.4713	.4719	.4726	.4732	.4738	.4744	.4750	.4756	.4761	.4767
2.0	.4772	.4778	.4783	.4788	.4793	.4798	.4803	.4808	.4812	.4817
2.1	.4821	.4826	.4830	.4834	.4838	.4842	.4846	.4850	.4854	.4857
2.2	.4861	.4864	.4868	.4871	.4875	.4878	.4881	.4884	.4887	.4890
2.3	.4893	.4896	.4898	.4901	.4904	.4906	.4909	.4911	.4913	.4916
2.4	.4918	.4920	.4922	.4925	.4927	.4929	.4931	.4932	.4934	.4936
2.5	.4938	.4940	.4941	.4943	.4945	.4946	.4948	.4949	.4951	.4952
2.6	.4953	.4955	.4956	.4957	.4959	.4960	.4961	.4962	.4963	.4964
2.7	.4965	.4966	.4967	.4968	.4969	.4970	.4971	.4972	.4973	.4974
2.8	.4974	.4975	.4976	.4977	.4977	.4978	.4979	.4979	.4980	.4981
2.9	.4981	.4982	.4982	.4983	.4984	.4984	.4985	.4985	.4986	.4986
3.0	.4987	.4987	.4987	.4988	.4988	.4989	.4989	.4989	.4990	.4990

TABLE 2

The t-distribution

Values of t for specified probabilities α.

Degrees of freedom	α =0.10	=0.05	=0.025	=0.01	= 0.005
1	3.078	6.314	12.706	31.821	63.657
2	1.886	2.920	4.303	6.965	9.925
3	1.638	2.353	3.182	4.541	5.841
4	1.533	2.132	2.776	3.747	4.604
5	1.476	2.015	2.571	3.365	4.032
6	1.440	1.943	2.447	3.143	3.707
7	1.415	1.895	2.365	2.998	3.499
8	1.397	1.860	2.306	2.896	3.355
9	1.383	1.833	2.262	2.821	3.250
10	1.372	1.812	2.228	2.764	3.169
11	1.363	1.796	2.201	2.718	3.106
12	1.356	1.782	2.179	2.681	3.055
13	1.350	1.771	2.160	2.650	3.012
14	1.345	1.761	2.145	2.624	2.977
15	1.341	1.753	2.131	2.602	2.947
16	1.337	1.746	2.120	2.583	2.921
17	1.333	1.740	2.110	2.567	2.898
18	1.330	1.734	2.101	2.552	2.878
19	1.328	1.729	2.093	2.539	2.861
20	1.325	1.725	2.086	2.528	2.845
21	1.323	1.721	2.080	2.518	2.831
22	1.321	1.717	2.074	2.508	2.819
23	1.319	1.714	2.069	2.500	2.807
24	1.318	1.711	2.064	2.492	2.797
25	1.316	1.708	2.060	2.485	2.787
26	1.315	1.706	2.056	2.479	2.779
27	1.314	1.703	2.052	2.473	2.771
28	1.313	1.701	2.048	2.467	2.763
29	1.311	1.699	2.045	2.462	2.756
30	1.310	1.697	2.042	2.457	2.750
∞	1.282	1.645	1.960	2.326	2.576

Acknowledgements: Tables 1. and 2. Adapted, with permission, from R. A. Fisher and F. Yates, *Statistical Tables*, 6th edition (Edinburgh: Oliver and Boyd, 1963; rptd. London: Longman, 1973).

TABLE 3

THE F - DISTRIBUTION

Level of significance = 0.05

Degrees of freedom in denominator (n-k-1)	Degrees of freedom in numerator (k)										
	1	2	3	4	5	6	7	8	9	10	∞
1	161	200	216	225	230	234	237	239	241	242	254
2	18.5	19.0	19.2	19.2	19.3	19.3	19.4	19.4	19.4	19.4	19.5
3	10.13	9.55	9.28	9.12	9.01	8.94	8.89	8.85	8.81	8.79	8.53
4	7.71	6.94	6.59	6.39	6.26	6.16	6.09	6.04	6.00	5.96	5.63
5	6.61	5.79	5.41	5.19	5.05	4.95	4.88	4.82	4.77	4.74	4.37
6	5.99	5.14	4.76	4.53	4.39	4.28	4.21	4.15	4.10	4.06	3.67
7	5.59	4.74	4.35	4.12	3.97	3.87	3.79	3.73	3.68	3.64	3.23
8	5.32	4.46	4.07	3.84	3.69	3.58	3.50	3.44	3.39	3.35	2.93
9	5.12	4.26	3.86	3.63	3.48	3.37	3.29	3.23	3.18	3.14	2.71
10	4.96	4.10	3.71	3.48	3.33	3.22	3.14	3.07	3.02	2.98	2.54
11	4.84	3.98	3.59	3.36	3.20	3.09	3.01	2.95	2.90	2.85	2.40
12	4.75	3.89	3.49	3.26	3.11	3.00	2.91	2.85	2.80	2.75	2.30
13	4.67	3.81	3.41	3.18	3.03	2.92	2.83	2.77	2.71	2.67	2.21
14	4.60	3.74	3.34	3.11	2.96	2.85	2.76	2.70	2.65	2.60	2.13
15	4.54	3.68	3.29	3.06	2.90	2.79	2.71	2.64	2.59	2.54	2.07
16	4.49	3.63	3.24	3.01	2.85	2.74	2.66	2.59	2.54	2.49	2.01
17	4.45	3.59	3.20	2.96	2.81	2.70	2.61	2.55	2.49	2.45	1.96
18	4.41	3.55	3.16	2.93	2.77	2.66	2.58	2.51	2.46	2.41	1.92
19	4.38	3.52	3.13	2.90	2.74	2.63	2.54	2.48	2.42	2.38	1.88
20	4.35	3.49	3.10	2.87	2.71	2.60	2.51	2.45	2.39	2.35	1.84
25	4.24	3.39	2.99	2.76	2.60	2.49	2.40	2.34	2.28	2.24	1.71
30	4.17	3.32	2.92	2.69	2.53	2.42	2.33	2.27	2.21	2.16	1.62
40	4.08	3.23	2.84	2.61	2.45	2.34	2.25	2.18	2.12	2.08	1.51
60	4.00	3.15	2.76	2.53	2.37	2.25	2.17	2.10	2.04	1.99	1.39
∞	3.84	3.00	2.60	2.37	2.21	2.10	2.01	1.94	1.88	1.83	1.00

Acknowledgements: Abridged from M. Merrington and C. M. Thompson, 'Tables of percentage points of the inverted beta (F) distribution', *Biometrika*, Vol. 33 (1943), by permission of the *Biometrika* trustees.

TABLE 4

The Durbin-Watson Statistic

Level of significance = 0.05

no. of observations	no. of independent variables									
	1		2		3		4		5	
	d_L	d_U	d_L	d_U	d_L	d_U	d_L	d_U	d_L	d_U
15	1.08	1.36	0.95	1.54	0.82	1.75	0.69	1.97	0.56	2.21
20	1.20	1.41	1.10	1.54	1.00	1.68	0.90	1.83	0.79	1.99
25	1.29	1.45	1.21	1.55	1.12	1.66	1.04	1.77	0.95	1.89
30	1.35	1.49	1.28	1.57	1.21	1.65	1.14	1.74	1.07	1.83
40	1.44	1.54	1.39	1.60	1.34	1.66	1.29	1.72	1.23	1.79
50	1.50	1.59	1.46	1.63	1.42	1.67	1.38	1.72	1.34	1.77
60	1.55	1.62	1.51	1.65	1.48	1.69	1.44	1.73	1.41	1.77
80	1.61	1.66	1.59	1.69	1.56	1.72	1.53	1.74	1.51	1.77
100	1.65	1.69	1.63	1.72	1.61	1.74	1.59	1.76	1.57	1.78

Note: For values of d lying between d_L and d_U, the hypothesis of serial correlation can be neither confirmed nor rejected at the 0·05 level of significance.

Acknowledgements: Abridged from J. Durbin and G. S. Watson, "Testing for serial correlation in least-squares regression', *Biometrika*, Vol. 38 (1951), by permission of the *Biometrika* trustees.

Index